125 best
chocolate chip
recipes

125 best
chocolate chip
recipes

JULIE HASSON

125 Best Chocolate Chip Recipes
Text copyright © 2003 Julie Hasson
Photographs copyright © 2003 Robert Rose Inc.

For complete cataloguing information, see page 182.

Disclaimer
The recipes in this book have been carefully tested by our kitchen and our tasters. To the best of our knowledge, they are safe and nutritious for ordinary use and users. For those people with food or other allergies, or who have special food requirements or health issues, please read the suggested contents of each recipe carefully and determine whether or not they may create a problem for you. All recipes are used at the risk of the consumer.

We cannot be responsible for any hazards, loss or damage that may occur as a result of any recipe use.

For those with special needs, allergies, requirements or health problems, in the event of any doubt, please contact your medical adviser prior to the use of any recipe.

Design & Production: PageWave Graphics Inc.
Editor: Carol Sherman
Copy Editor: Julia Armstrong
Recipe Tester: Jennifer MacKenzie
Photography: Mark T. Shapiro
Food Stylist: Kate Bush
Props Stylist: Charlene Erricson
Color Scans: Colour Technologies

The publisher and author wish to express their appreciation to the following suppliers of props used in the food photography:

DISHES, LINENS, GLASSWARE & ACCESSORIES

Caban
396 St. Clair Avenue West
Toronto, Ontario, M5P 3N3
Tel: (416) 654-3316
www.caban.ca

Homefront
371 Eglinton Avenue West
Toronto, Ontario, M5N 1A3
Tel: (416) 488-3189
www.homefrontshop.com

The Kitchen & Glass Place
840 Yonge Street
Toronto, Ontario, M4W 2H1
Tel: (416) 927-9925

FLATWARE

Gourmet Settings Inc.
245 West Beaver Creek Rd., Unit 10
Richmond Hill, Ontario, L4B 1L1
Tel: 1-800-551-2649
www.gourmetsettings.com

We acknowledge the financial support of the Government of Canada through the Book Publishing Industry Development Program (BPIDP) for our publishing activities.

Published by: Robert Rose Inc.
120 Eglinton Ave. E., Suite 800, Toronto, Ontario, Canada M4P 1E2
Tel: (416) 322-6552 Fax: (416) 322-6936

Printed in Canada
1 2 3 4 5 6 7   GP   09 08 07 06 05 04 03

Contents

Acknowledgments

MANY HEARTFELT THANKS TO everyone who helped make this book come to life. First of all, a titanic thanks to Lisa Ekus, the agent of all agents, who helped me take a cool idea from concept to reality. Thank you for all of your hard work and belief in this cookbook writer.

Thank you to Bob Dees at Robert Rose for his incredible faith in this project. This has been a wonderful experience! Thanks also to Carol Sherman, my editor, for all of her input and hard work on this manuscript. Thanks to Jennifer MacKenzie for her excellent recipe testing and recommendations. Thanks also to Mark Shapiro for his fine photography and Kate Bush for her great food styling. Thanks to Andrew Smith, Daniella Zanchetta and everyone at PageWave Graphics. Thank you to everyone at Robert Rose for working so hard on this book and doing such a great job!

I want to thank my awesome husband, Jay, for his undying support, humor and love. You have helped make all of my dreams come true. Thank you to my beautiful children, Sydney and Noah, for tasting thousands of recipes, even when you thought that you couldn't possibly taste another bite. I couldn't have done this without all of you!

Thank you to my mom for sharing her joy of cooking and love of food. You started me on this delicious journey, and I have never looked back. Thank you, Jon, for being such a cool brother and always loving my cooking. Thank you, Louie, for your love and support. Thank you to my wonderful crew of taste testers: the Thorntons, the Riebes, the Bussel-Smiths, the Goldsteins, Mrs. March's sixth grade class, Mrs. McCrea's third grade class and the rest of the gang who shared in the chocolate chip extravaganza.

Introduction

OVER THE PAST 14 YEARS, I have worked as a pastry chef, caterer, recipe developer and writer. Life has taken me down many interesting paths, juggling work, family, business and other responsibilities along the way. But through it all, food has always been the focus. Although I have a great reputation for my cooking, my desserts take on a life all their own.

After cooking school, I worked in several restaurants and bakeries in Los Angeles. When I was ready to branch out on my own, my husband, Jay, and I opened a bakery in Los Angeles called *Baby Cakes*. At that time, the coffeehouse boom had just started, and we supplied coffeehouses and restaurants with biscotti, cakes, cookies and specialty desserts. Jay and I have owned and operated a catering and baking company in Boise, Idaho, for the past six years. I also regularly teach cooking classes and contribute articles and recipes to several magazines. I have included several of the popular recipes from these articles in this book, as well as many of the most-requested recipes and best-selling items from my bakery.

From years of commercial baking, I have learned to streamline my recipes. I take them to their basic form — without sacrificing taste or flavor — eliminating the intimidation factor. By simplifying complicated techniques, the preparation and baking time are decreased significantly. Most of these recipes are designed for maximum impression with minimum fuss, and they can be thrown together in a matter of minutes. Take some time to acquaint yourself with the list of tools, equipment and ingredients on the following pages. Make a list of all the things you'll need to round out your cabinets and pantry, then go shopping. That way, whenever the spirit moves you, you can just pull out the cooking paraphernalia and go to town. And last, but not least, invite children into the kitchen. They will become your greatest fans. Who knows — with any luck, one day they may even cook for you. Have fun!

— Julie Hasson

TOOLS AND EQUIPMENT FOR PERFECT DESSERTS

In the grand world of kitchen equipment, there are definitely items that make baking a breeze. Certainly, you can make do with a large mixing bowl, a wooden spoon and a sturdy baking sheet. And, in some cases, I believe that simplicity is better. But drawing on my experience in professional kitchens and my obsession with kitchen equipment catalogs, here's a list of equipment that I believe will make everyone a professional in the kitchen.

MEASURING EQUIPMENT

Cookie/ice cream scoops: Available in a variety of sizes, these are a blessing in the kitchen. Use scoops to measure batter and dough evenly so that every cookie and muffin will turn out the same size. Plus, using a scoop will save you quite a bit of time.

Dry measuring cups: This is the most accurate way to measure dry ingredients (with the exception of a digital scale). I like to use a good-quality set of metal nesting measuring cups that come in a variety of measurements. When measuring, always remember to spoon your dry ingredients into the cup and level the top by scraping across it with the flat side of a knife or skewer. This will give you an accurate measurement.

Liquid measuring cups: The most accurate way to measure liquid ingredients is in glass or plastic liquid measuring cups with a lip or spout. I like to keep a variety of sizes in my kitchen for baking. Glass measuring cups are also ideal for melting chocolate chips in the microwave (see Microwave oven, page 11, for instructions).

Measuring spoons: This is the most accurate way to measure small amounts of both liquid and dry ingredients. Look for a metal set that ranges from $\frac{1}{8}$ tsp (0.5 mL) to 1 tbsp (15 mL).

Mixing bowls: A nesting set (or two or three) of mixing bowls is a must in the dessert kitchen. I like to have both stainless steel and ceramic, depending on the mixing job. Stainless steel bowls work best for whipping cream, ceramic ones for cookie and cake batters.

HAND TOOLS

Microplane® zester/grater: This tool makes quick work of removing and grating citrus zest. Just rub it over the surface of oranges, lemons and limes, carefully removing the colored peel.

Rubber spatulas: The new heat-safe, silicone spatulas are heatproof to 600°F (300°C). They are a boon to bakers as they scrape a bowl clean with ease. They are dishwasher-safe and can be used for stove-top cooking as well.

Sifter or strainer: This is an important tool for sifting dry ingredients or dusting a dessert with confectioner's (icing) sugar.

Whisk: The most important tool for cream, eggs, batter and anything else that requires whisking.

BAKING EQUIPMENT

Baking pans: You will need a variety of sizes of pans to make the desserts in this book. Always invest in heavier, quality pans as they conduct heat more efficiently. Here's a list of some basic-size pans that I use frequently: 9-by 5-inch (2 L) metal loaf pan, 8-inch (2 L) square metal pan, 13-by 9-inch (3 L) baking pan, muffin tins, Madeleine tins, rimmed baking sheets (also known as jelly-roll pans), 10-inch (3 L) Bundt pan, 9-inch (23 cm) springform pan and 9-inch (23 cm) tart pan.

Baking sheets: These are key pieces of equipment in the dessert kitchen. Look for good-quality, heavy-duty construction and feel.

You can often purchase them bundled in groups of two or three at large warehouse stores. A good-quality pan is definitely worth the small investment.

Cooling rack: A wire cooling rack elevates baking pans or baked goods so that air can circulate around them.

Nonstick saucepans and skillets: Look for good quality in a nonstick pan; there are big differences in quality. I personally like a saucepan that has a nice heavy feel to it yet releases food with ease. You will love making custards, puddings and sauces in nonstick saucepans. They are not a must, but they certainly aid in cooking and cleanup.

Parchment paper: This grease and heat-resistant paper is used to line baking sheets. It keeps your cookies and cakes from sticking and burning (unless you overbake them) and makes cleanup easy. This is the number one item on my list for baking. It is sometimes labeled "baking paper" and is stocked with other food wraps in the grocery store or in the baking section.

ELECTRIC EQUIPMENT

Blender: This is a must for smoothies and milkshakes. Try to find a blender that has an ice-crushing button, which also works well for frozen fruit and chocolate chips.

Food processor: This machine is essential for chopping nuts, chocolate chips, dried fruit and cookie crumbs, and for making the most delectable scones imaginable! I recommend the KitchenAid® and Cuisinart® brands. They will last forever and do a more consistent job than less expensive types.

Hand mixer: This is a great tool for quickly whipping cream and egg whites.

Immersion/stick blender: I love immersion/stick blenders. They blend quickly with a minimum of mess, making them ideal for sauces, dressings and whipped cream. Braun® and KitchenAid® are two very good brands.

Microwave oven: A microwave oven is definitely a plus in the dessert kitchen. I use it extensively to melt chocolate, heat cream and soften butter. (You can also use a double boiler to melt chocolate.) To melt chocolate in a microwave oven: In a large microwave-safe bowl (preferably a large glass measuring cup), melt chocolate chips and shortening (or cream or butter) on High, uncovered, for 1 to 2 minutes, stirring every 30 seconds, until chocolate is shiny and almost melted. Stir until smooth. Be careful not to overheat or cook the chocolate too long as it burns easily. I have tested the recipes in this book using a 1,000-watt microwave oven.

Oven: It really doesn't matter whether you use a gas or electric oven for baking. But do make sure that the oven is calibrated (precisely adjusted) so that it bakes evenly and at the required temperature. The recipes in this book were tested using a conventional electric oven.

A great way to make sure your oven is baking at the correct temperature is to use an oven thermometer. Leave it in your oven at all times as it can withstand high temperatures. Before placing your items in the oven to bake, check the thermometer to make sure that it is at the correct temperature.

Stand mixer: This isn't a must for all recipes, but it sure makes life a lot easier. I recommend a heavy, sturdy stand mixer, such as KitchenAid®. They last for years and now come in some beautiful colors as well. This is your best bet for batters, whipped cream or eggs.

COMMON INGREDIENTS

I have included a list of common ingredients used in this book. I recommend stocking your pantry with many of these items to make baking a snap. If you have to run to the store every time you want to make a batch of chocolate chip cookies, you will think twice about baking. My trick is to always have certain items on hand so that at any given moment I can whip together a recipe. With items such as chocolate chips, flour, oats, sugar, butter, eggs, milk and nuts in your pantry or fridge, you can throw together scones, cookies, ice creams, puddings, cakes and other treats in mere minutes.

BUTTER

I recommend using unsalted butter unless otherwise specified in the recipe. The quality is better, the flavor purer, and you can control the saltiness of your recipe. If you only have salted butter in the house, you can substitute it in most cases in these recipes. Just be sure to omit all other salt called for in the recipe.

Margarine cannot be substituted for butter in these recipes, unless noted in a particular recipe. To bring cold butter to room temperature in a hurry, use a microwave oven. I usually set it on Medium for 20 seconds, making sure not to melt the butter.

CHOCOLATE

Chocolate chips: When using chocolate chips in these recipes, use good-quality, real semisweet chocolate chips. The better the quality, the better the taste of the final product. I recommend keeping a big bag of chocolate chips in the pantry at all times so that you can be ready to go with any of these recipes. Large bags of chocolate chips are available at club stores in most cities.

Unsweetened chocolate: I like to use unsweetened chocolate in tandem with chocolate chips as it can deepen and enhance the chocolate flavor.

Baking chocolate and bittersweet chocolate cannot be substituted for the unsweetened chocolate in these recipes.

Semisweet and bittersweet chocolate bars: I like to keep a few on hand because if you are out of chocolate chips, they make a very tasty stand-in. Coarsely chop the bars with a sharp chef's knife and use, measure for measure, as you would chocolate chips. Valrhona and Scharffen Berger are two very good brands. They are becoming more readily available at better grocery and health food stores.

Cocoa powder: I use unsweetened Dutch-process cocoa powder in my baking. It is a dark, rich cocoa powder that has been processed with alkali, which neutralizes its natural acidity. Cocoa powder always needs to be sifted before use because it can be very lumpy, which makes it difficult to incorporate. Use a fine-meshed sieve to remove any lumps before adding cocoa powder to other dry ingredients. Pernigotti, Van Leer, Droste and Guittard are all excellent brands of Dutch-process cocoa powder.

COFFEE

Ground coffee: The recipes in this book were tested using French roast coffee beans, finely ground. To make strong-brewed coffee, use a ratio of 2 tbsp (25 mL) finely ground coffee per 6 oz (175 mL) water. This ratio will yield a strong yet flavorful brewed coffee.

Instant coffee granules: This is an easy way to add coffee flavor without brewing coffee. The crystals dissolve instantly in hot liquid.

DAIRY

Buttermilk: Buttermilk is made from low-fat or nonfat milk that has had a bacterial culture added (somewhat like yogurt), creating a slightly tangy, creamy product. It gives baked goods a delicious flavor and moist texture. If you are out of buttermilk, you can make your own sour milk: Pour 1 tbsp (15 mL) lemon juice or white vinegar into a measuring cup. Add enough milk to make 1 cup (250 mL). Let stand for about 5 minutes before using.

Milk: The recipes in this book were tested using whole milk, but 2% is also acceptable.

Cream: Look for whipping (35%) cream or heavy whipping cream as well as half-and-half (10%) cream. They will keep, refrigerated, for quite a while. For better flavor, look for brands from organic dairies. I always have cream on hand as it is perfect for last-minute desserts, from ice cream to truffles.

Cream cheese: Cream cheese is a fresh cheese made from cow's milk. For quality and consistency, you are better off sticking with name brands and avoiding the "spreadable" nonfat or low-fat varieties in baking.

Sour cream: The addition of sour cream, a high-fat version of buttermilk, helps to produce rich and tender results. Light, low-fat and nonfat varieties are not interchangeable with regular sour cream in these recipes.

Sweetened condensed milk: Sweetened condensed milk is made from sweetened nonfat or whole milk, with all of the water removed. It is not the same as evaporated milk and cannot be used interchangeably.

DRIED FRUIT

Dried fruit is great to keep on hand for baking. Certain fruits, such as dried cherries, cranberries and apricots, go especially well with chocolate.

EGGS

The recipes in this book were tested using large eggs. I generally suggest bringing your eggs to room temperature for baking, but in most of these recipes you can use chilled eggs if need be.

EXTRACTS

Always use pure extracts in your baking as they are superior in quality and flavor to artificial flavorings. Imitation vanilla is made from synthetic substances, which imitates part of the natural vanilla smell and flavor.

FLAVORED BAKING CHIPS

Some of the recipes in this book call for flavored chips, such as mint, butterscotch, milk or white baking chips. Do not substitute these chips for semisweet chocolate chips.

FLOUR

All of the recipes in this book were tested using unbleached all-purpose flour, which I feel is a healthier alternative. Bleached flour has been chemically bleached and bromated; I prefer not to use it. You can, however, substitute bleached flour for unbleached flour in these recipes.

LIQUEURS

I love to keep a stash of different-flavored liqueurs and spirits on hand for cooking and baking. Some key ones are rum, Triple Sec (orange brandy), Kirsch (cherry brandy), coffee liqueur and brandy. Airline-size bottles are ideal if you don't have full-size bottles on hand.

NONSTICK COOKING SPRAY

This is a must in the dessert kitchen. Nonstick cooking spray is a quick way to grease your pans and is more reliable than butter or oil. Choose a spray that is unflavored.

NUTS

The recipes in this book use a variety of nuts, such as almonds, walnuts and pecans. Store nuts in the freezer to keep them fresh, as they can become rancid very quickly. Toast them for the fullest flavor. *To toast nuts:* Preheat oven to 350°F (180°C). Spread nuts on a foil- or parchment-lined baking sheet and bake for 5 to 7 minutes or until lightly browned and fragrant.

OATS

Oats are a whole grain that are usually purchased "rolled." Buy quick-cooking and old-fashioned varieties to use in cookies, bars, cakes and granola. They are not interchangeable in recipes.

OIL

The recipes in this book call for vegetable oil. I prefer canola oil, but you can substitute vegetable or soy oil should you desire. You will want to use a light, flavorless oil, which is why olive oil is not interchangeable.

SALT

All of the recipes in this book were tested with plain table salt. Although I like kosher or sea salt on my food, I prefer to use table salt for baking.

SHORTENING

When the recipe calls for shortening, always use solid white vegetable shortening. Do not substitute margarine or butter for shortening.

SPICES

Certain spices are a must-have in the dessert kitchen, such as ground cinnamon, ground ginger, ground allspice, ground cloves and ground cardamom. Spices tend to go stale quickly, so discard if they are no longer fragrant.

SUGAR

Granulated sugar: A highly refined sugar that comes from sugar beets or sugar cane.

Confectioner's (icing) sugar: Sugar that has been "powdered" or pulverized and mixed with a small amount of cornstarch.

Brown sugar: Granulated sugar mixed with molasses.

Superfine or baker's sugar: Superfine or baker's sugar is ultra-fine granulated sugar, which dissolves very quickly in liquid. If you cannot find it in your local grocery store, you can make your own: process granulated sugar in a food processor until very finely ground.

Corn syrup: This thick, sweet syrup is made from cornstarch. Corn syrup can be purchased in both light and dark varieties.

Honey: Bees make honey from flower nectar. When using honey as a sweetener, the darker the honey the stronger the flavor. A light honey is preferable when you don't want to overwhelm the flavors of a dessert. Do not substitute honey for sugar unless called for in a specific recipe.

Molasses: The liquid left after pure sugar has been extracted from sugar cane or sugar beets. There are several varieties of molasses, such as sulphured and unsulphured, fancy, cooking and blackstrap. The recipes in this book were tested with light unsulphured or fancy molasses.

TIPS FOR BETTER RESULTS

Here are a few tips to make you a professional in the kitchen.

- Remember that cooking and baking is fun! I like to look at it as a spiritual retreat from the chaos and stress of our everyday lives.

- Read through the entire recipe before starting. That way, you know both the steps and ingredients in the recipe before you begin.

- Place your baking racks as close to the center of the oven as possible.

- Make sure that your oven is fully preheated before baking. It will probably take between 10 and 15 minutes to preheat, depending on your oven.

- Line your baking sheets with parchment paper for blissful baking. It will keep your baked goods from sticking, making cleanup a snap.

- When measuring dry ingredients, always spoon them into dry measuring cups or spoons, then level the top by scraping across it with the flat side of a knife or skewer.

- Use a cookie scoop for consistency. Your cookies will bake more evenly if they are all the same size. A cookie scoop will also give your muffins, cookies and scones a professional appearance.

- Make sure that your cookies and scones are evenly spaced on the pan to allow room for spreading and rising; place them 2 to 3 inches (5 to 7.5 cm) apart.

- If baking more than one pan of cookies or bars at a time, rotate your baking sheets halfway through baking.

- If baking more than one pan of cookies at a time, baking will take slightly longer. Adjust your baking time accordingly, relying on visual signs of doneness; generally, you will need to bake about 5 minutes longer.

- Let your baking pans cool thoroughly before reusing for your next batch.

Beverages

Blended Mocha Frappé

Here is your chance to be your own barista. I live on these frosty coffee-flavored shakes during the hot summer months. You can make this blended coffee creation — found at coffeehouses around the globe — at home for a fraction of the cost.

Variation

Reduce sugar and add your choice of flavored syrups, such as hazelnut, almond or caramel, to taste.

2 cups	ice cubes	500 mL
1 cup	milk	250 mL
1/2 cup	strong brewed coffee, chilled	125 mL
1/3 cup	superfine sugar	75 mL
1/3 cup	table (18%) cream	75 mL
1/3 cup	semisweet chocolate chips	75 mL
2 tbsp	instant coffee granules	25 mL

1. In a blender, combine ice, milk, chilled coffee, sugar, cream, chocolate chips and instant coffee granules. Blend until smooth and frothy.

2. Pour into glasses and serve immediately.

Cookies-and-Cream Shake

This is a fun shake, especially for those diehard fans of cookies and milk. And when they're served this way, you won't be chasing broken cookie pieces around the cup of milk.

Variation

Substitute chocolate chip cookies for the chocolate sandwich cookies.

6	scoops vanilla ice cream	6
1 cup	milk	250 mL
¼ cup	semisweet chocolate chips	50 mL
4	cream-filled chocolate sandwich cookies	4
	Whipped cream (optional)	

1. In a blender, combine ice cream, milk, chocolate chips and chocolate sandwich cookies. Blend until frothy.

2. Pour into glasses and serve immediately with straws. Garnish with a dollop of whipped cream, if desired.

Chocolate Malted

When you're in the mood for something sweet and creamy, give this beverage a try. It's a smooth drink of malted milk powder, ice cream and chocolate chips.

6	scoops vanilla ice cream	6
¾ cup	milk	175 mL
½ cup	semisweet chocolate chips	125 mL
3 tbsp	malted milk powder	45 mL
	Whipped cream (optional)	

1. In a blender, combine ice cream, milk, chocolate chips and malted milk powder. Blend until smooth.

2. Pour into glasses and serve immediately with straws. Garnish the shake with a dollop of whipped cream, if desired.

Chocolate Caramel Cream Shake

I am a huge caramel fan. The combination of caramel, Irish Cream and chocolate makes this shake one of my faves.

Tip

For a thicker shake, add additional ice cream.

8	large scoops vanilla ice cream	8
¾ cup	milk	175 mL
¼ cup	Chocolate Caramel Sauce (see recipe, page 166) or store-bought caramel sauce	50 mL
¼ cup	semisweet chocolate chips	50 mL
1 tbsp	Irish Cream liqueur	15 mL
	Whipped cream (optional)	

1. In a blender, combine ice cream, milk, chocolate caramel sauce, chocolate chips and liqueur. Blend until smooth.

2. Pour into glasses and serve immediately with straws. Garnish with a dollop of whipped cream, if desired.

Chocolatini

This is a really fun cocktail to serve — decadent and equally delicious to drink. Not too sweet, even with the chocolate touch, this is the queen of cocktails. I dedicate this recipe to my sister-in-law Randie, who, like this drink, is always the "belle of the ball."

Tip

Store vodka in the freezer to keep it cold and ready for perfect martinis.

Variation

Substitute raspberry liqueur for the cassis.

Two martini glasses

2 tbsp	confectioner's (icing) sugar, sifted	25 mL
	Ice cubes	
3 oz	cold vodka	90 mL
1 tbsp	chocolate syrup	15 mL
1 tbsp	crème de cassis liqueur	15 mL
10	semisweet chocolate chips	10

1. Place martini glasses in the freezer for 10 minutes to chill. Spread confectioner's sugar on a small saucer. Dip the rims of the chilled glasses in the confectioner's sugar to coat lightly.

2. Fill a cocktail shaker with ice cubes. Pour vodka, chocolate syrup and crème de cassis over the ice.

3. Shake mixture until cocktail shaker becomes frosty. Strain into prepared glasses. Garnish each drink with 5 chocolate chips.

Cosmic Coffee with Chocolate Chips and Chantilly Cream

This is a really fun way to end a dinner. Just make sure you save some room. Once you have tried this beverage, you will never want plain, boring coffee again.

Tips

Garnish each mug of coffee with a cinnamon stick. It adds a great flavor to the coffee. Another fun way to serve this coffee is to offer flavored coffee syrups in addition to the whipped cream and chocolate chips. Hazelnut, peppermint, vanilla and almond would all be equally delicious.

This recipe can be doubled.

Variation

Substitute espresso for the brewed coffee.

1 cup	whipping (35%) cream	250 mL
2 tsp	confectioner's (icing) sugar, sifted	10 mL
1/2 tsp	vanilla	2 mL
4 cups	strong brewed coffee	1 L
1/3 cup	semisweet chocolate chips	75 mL

1. In a large bowl, combine cream, confectioner's sugar and vanilla. Beat until soft peaks form.

2. Pour the hot coffee into mugs. Dollop with whipped cream. Top with chocolate chips.

Hot Chocolate Chai Latte

I love to pack a Thermos of this creamy tea for winter picnics or early morning outings. It's a fun alternative to coffee or hot chocolate.

2 cups	water	500 mL
1/4 cup	loose-leaf black tea	50 mL
2 cups	milk	500 mL
1/3 cup	granulated sugar	75 mL
1 tsp	ground cinnamon	5 mL
1/2 tsp	ground allspice	2 mL
1/2 tsp	ground cardamom	2 mL
1/2 cup	semisweet chocolate chips	125 mL
	Whipped cream (optional)	

1. In a large saucepan over medium heat, bring water to a simmer. Remove from heat and add loose tea. Let steep for 5 minutes.

2. Add milk, sugar, cinnamon, allspice and cardamom. Return saucepan to medium heat and bring to a simmer for several minutes or until steaming. Remove from heat and strain into a measuring cup with spout.

3. Whisk in chocolate chips and serve at once in mugs. Garnish with whipped cream, if desired.

Hot Spiced Chocolate

Hot chocolate has never tasted so good. Honest! Four little ingredients combine in this recipe to concoct one powerhouse beverage.

Tip

You can garnish this steaming hot chocolate with marshmallows or a dollop of whipped cream. Personally, I love it just the way it is.

3 cups	milk	750 mL
1/2 cup	whipping (35%) cream	125 mL
1 cup	semisweet chocolate chips	250 mL
1/4 tsp	ground cinnamon	1 mL

1. In a medium saucepan over medium-high heat, bring milk and cream to a simmer.

2. Remove saucepan from heat and whisk in chocolate chips and cinnamon, if using, until smooth.

3. Serve hot chocolate in mugs.

Strawberry Chip "Moo-thie"

Smoothies have been around for many years but recently have become very popular. This delicious version combines strawberries, banana and, of course, chocolate chips.

Tip
If you prefer a sweeter smoothie, add more sugar to taste.

1¼ cups	milk	300 mL
5 oz	frozen unsweetened strawberries (about 1⅓ cups/325 mL)	150 g
½	banana	½
2	scoops vanilla ice cream	2
¼ cup	semisweet chocolate chips	50 mL
3 tbsp	superfine sugar	45 mL
	Fresh strawberries (optional)	

1. In a blender, combine milk, strawberries, banana, ice cream, chocolate chips and sugar. Blend until smooth.

2. Pour into glasses and serve immediately with straws. Garnish with a fresh strawberry, if desired.

Breakfast

Apricot Chip Scones

These scones go together beautifully in the food processor, which effortlessly cuts the butter into the flour, resulting in the most tender and flaky scones imaginable.

Tips

This recipe can be doubled.

These scones are best served the day they are made.

Preheat oven to 425°F (220°C)

Baking sheets, lined with parchment paper or greased

3 cups	all-purpose flour	750 mL
1/3 cup	granulated sugar	75 mL
2 1/2 tsp	baking powder	12 mL
1/2 tsp	baking soda	2 mL
1/2 tsp	salt	2 mL
1 1/2 cups	unsalted butter, chilled and cut into pieces	375 mL
1 cup	buttermilk	250 mL
2/3 cup	dried apricots, snipped into strips	150 mL
1/2 cup	semisweet chocolate chips	125 mL

Topping

1 tbsp	granulated sugar	15 mL
1/4 tsp	ground cinnamon	1 mL
2 tbsp	whipping (35%) cream	25 mL
	Confectioner's (icing) sugar, for dusting	

1. In a food processor fitted with a metal blade, combine flour, sugar, baking powder, baking soda and salt. Pulse for 5 seconds. Add butter and pulse using on/off motion until mixture resembles coarse meal. Add buttermilk and pulse just until the dough forms a ball. Stir in apricots and chocolate chips.

2. Scooping dough with rounded 1/4-cup (50 mL) ice cream scoop or measuring cup, place balls of dough on prepared baking sheets, about 3 inches (7.5 cm) apart.

3. *Topping:* In a small bowl, mix together sugar and cinnamon. Brush tops of scones with cream and sprinkle with cinnamon-sugar topping. Bake in preheated oven for 18 to 20 minutes or until crusty and golden brown. Transfer scones to a rack to cool. Dust lightly with confectioner's sugar before serving.

Chocolate Chip Cherry Breakfast Biscuits

Makes 8 biscuits

These are amazingly delicious biscuits. I wanted to create a recipe for a cream-style biscuit that you could eat for breakfast, studded with dried cherries and chocolate chips. This recipe is it.

Tips

This recipe can be doubled.

The biscuits will stay fresh for several days if stored in an airtight container.

Ragged dough looks moistened but doesn't form a ball.

Variation

Substitute ½ cup (125 mL) dried cranberries and 1 tsp (5 mL) grated orange zest for the dried cherries.

Preheat oven to 400°F (200°C)
Baking sheet, lined with parchment paper

2¼ cups	all-purpose flour	550 mL
⅓ cup	dried sour cherries	75 mL
⅓ cup	semisweet chocolate chips	75 mL
¼ cup	granulated sugar	50 mL
1 tbsp	baking powder	15 mL
¼ tsp	salt	1 mL
1¼ cups	whipping (35%) cream	300 mL

Topping

2 tbsp	whipping (35%) cream	25 mL
	Confectioner's (icing) sugar, for dusting	

1. In a large bowl, mix together flour, cherries, chocolate chips, sugar, baking powder and salt.

2. Pour in cream, stirring just until dough is soft and ragged (see Tips, left).

3. Turn out dough onto a lightly floured work surface and gently shape into an 8-by 6-inch (20 by 15 cm) rectangle. Using a sharp knife, cut into 8 wedges. Transfer biscuits to prepared baking sheet, making sure they do not touch or overlap.

4. *Topping:* Lightly brush tops with cream. Bake in preheated oven for about 20 minutes or until crisp and golden brown. Transfer biscuits to a rack to cool. Dust lightly with confectioner's sugar before serving.

Chocolate Chip Oat Breakfast Biscuits

This is a great-tasting way to get your oatmeal in the morning, as well as your chocolate fix. If you like scones, you will love these cream breakfast biscuits.

Tips

This recipe can be doubled.

The biscuits can also be patted out into a circle and cut into pie-shaped wedges or cut into hearts or circles with biscuit or cookie cutters.

Preheat oven to 400°F (200°C)
Baking sheet, lined with parchment paper

1½ cups	all-purpose flour	375 mL
¾ cup	old-fashioned rolled oats	175 mL
½ cup	semisweet chocolate chips	125 mL
¼ cup	granulated sugar	50 mL
1 tbsp	baking powder	15 mL
¼ tsp	salt	1 mL
1¼ cups	whipping (35%) cream	300 mL

Topping (optional)

2 tbsp	whipping (35%) cream	25 mL

Glaze

¾ cup	confectioner's (icing) sugar, sifted	175 mL
4 tsp	orange juice	20 mL

1. In a large bowl, mix together flour, oats, chocolate chips, sugar, baking powder and salt.

2. Stir in cream, mixing just until dough is soft and ragged (see Tips, page 31).

3. Turn out dough onto a lightly floured work surface and gently shape into an 8-by 6-inch (20 by 15 cm) rectangle. Using a sharp knife, cut into 8 wedges. Transfer biscuits to prepared baking sheet, making sure they do not touch or overlap.

4. *Topping:* Lightly brush the tops with cream. Bake in preheated oven for about 20 minutes or until crisp and golden brown. Transfer biscuits to a rack to cool.

5. *Glaze:* In a medium bowl, whisk together confectioner's sugar and orange juice until smooth. Dip tops of cooled biscuits in glaze or drizzle glaze over top. Let biscuits stand on a rack until glaze hardens.

Chocolate Malted *(page 22)*

Chocolate Almond Bread Spread

This is a delectable breakfast spread and dessert rolled into one. A protein and chocolate combination is a wonderful way to jump-start your day. Serve with bagels, scones or even on bread as a breakfast sandwich.

Tips

To toast almonds: Preheat oven to 350°F (180°C). Spread nuts on a baking sheet lined with foil or parchment. Bake for 5 to 7 minutes or until light brown and fragrant.

If you want to decrease the oil in this recipe, you can cut it down to 1 tsp (5 mL). Note, though, that the spread will be very thick and somewhat difficult to spread.

1 cup	whole almonds, toasted (see Tips, left)	250 mL
¾ cup	semisweet chocolate chips	175 mL
4 tsp	canola oil (see Tips, left)	20 mL
2 tsp	light corn syrup	10 mL
¼ tsp	salt	1 mL

1. In a food processor fitted with a metal blade, combine almonds and chocolate chips. Process for about 4 minutes (this will be very loud for the first minute or so), until mixture becomes smooth and almost forms a ball. With motor running, add oil, corn syrup and salt through the feed tube.

2. Transfer to a microwave-safe bowl. Cover and refrigerate for up to 2 days. Just before serving, warm spread in microwave on High for about 20 seconds, until spreadable.

Apricot Chip Scones (page 30)

Chocolate Chip Jammer Scones

These scones have been a part of my catering repertoire for years. I love the flavor of the baked raspberry jam with the chocolate chips. They are especially fun to serve on Valentine's Day or for a special brunch.

Tips

This recipe can be doubled.

These scones are best served the day they are made.

Variation

Substitute strawberry or cherry jam for the raspberry.

Preheat oven to 425°F (220°C)

Baking sheet, lined with parchment paper or lightly greased

¼ cup	raspberry jam	50 mL
¼ cup	semisweet chocolate chips	50 mL
3 cups	all-purpose flour	750 mL
¼ cup	granulated sugar	50 mL
2½ tsp	baking powder	12 mL
½ tsp	baking soda	2 mL
½ tsp	salt	2 mL
1½ cups	unsalted butter, chilled and cut into pieces	375 mL
¾ cup	buttermilk	175 mL

Topping

2 tbsp	whipping (35%) cream	25 mL
2 tbsp	granulated sugar	25 mL
	Confectioner's (icing) sugar, for dusting (optional)	

1. In a small bowl, mix together raspberry jam and chocolate chips. Set aside.

2. In a food processor fitted with a metal blade, combine flour, sugar, baking powder, baking soda and salt. Pulse for 5 seconds. Add butter and pulse using on/off motion until mixture resembles coarse meal.

3. Add buttermilk and pulse just until the dough forms a ball. Scooping dough with rounded ¼-cup (50 mL) ice cream scoop or measuring cup, place balls on prepared sheets, about 3 inches (7.5 cm) apart. Using your thumb, make a deep indentation on top of each scone. Place a scoop of the reserved raspberry mixture in each indentation.

4. *Topping:* Brush tops of scones with cream and sprinkle with sugar. Bake in preheated oven for about 20 minutes, until crusty and golden brown. Transfer scones to rack to cool. Dust lightly with confectioner's sugar before serving, if desired.

Chocolate Cherry Chip Granola

*This is definitely the
breakfast of champions.
It is also delicious as an
afternoon or midnight snack,
sprinkled over vanilla ice
cream or just eaten out of
the hand like a trail mix.*

Tip

Kitchen shears are a great
way to slice dried apricots
(or any dried fruit, for
that matter).

Variations

Substitute dried cranberries
for the cherries or vegetable
oil for the butter. If you use
oil instead of butter, the
texture will be the same, but
the granola will not have a
buttery taste.

Preheat oven to 350°F (180°C)
Rimmed baking sheet, lined with foil

4 cups	old-fashioned rolled oats	1 L
1 cup	almonds, sliced, slivered or chopped	250 mL
1/2 cup	packed light brown sugar	125 mL
2 tsp	ground cinnamon	10 mL
1/2 cup	unsalted butter, melted	125 mL
1/4 cup	liquid honey	50 mL
1 cup	semisweet chocolate chips	250 mL
1 cup	dried sour cherries	250 mL
1/2 cup	dried apricots, snipped into thin strips (see Tip, left)	125 mL

1. In a large bowl, toss together oats, almonds, brown sugar and cinnamon.

2. Whisk together melted butter and honey. Pour over oat mixture, mixing well until all the oats are coated.

3. Spread mixture onto prepared baking sheet. Bake in preheated oven, stirring occasionally, for 25 to 30 minutes or until golden brown. Remove from oven and let cool.

4. Place cooled oat mixture in a large bowl and toss with chocolate chips, dried cherries and dried apricots. Store in an airtight container for several weeks.

Chocolate Chip Hotcakes

Who wouldn't like a sprinkling of chocolate chips on their pancakes? When I tested this recipe on my children and their friends, my kitchen became eerily silent. Then, once the pancakes were devoured, they uttered three words: "More pancakes, please!"

Tips
These pancakes are wonderful served with maple or berry syrup.

This recipe can be halved for a smaller batch.

Variations
To make banana chocolate chip pancakes, sprinkle 1 cup (250 mL) banana slices on top of the pancakes along with the chocolate chips.

To make cinnamon chocolate pancakes, lightly dust with ground cinnamon after sprinkling with chocolate chips.

2 cups	all-purpose flour	500 mL
3 tbsp	granulated sugar	45 mL
2 tsp	baking powder	10 mL
1 tsp	baking soda	5 mL
$\frac{1}{4}$ tsp	salt	1 mL
2	eggs	2
2 cups	buttermilk	500 mL
2 tsp	vanilla	10 mL
	Unsalted butter, as needed	
$\frac{2}{3}$ cup	semisweet chocolate chips	150 mL

1. In a large bowl, combine flour, sugar, baking powder, baking soda and salt.

2. In a separate bowl, whisk together eggs, buttermilk and vanilla. Add buttermilk mixture to flour mixture, stirring just until combined. (The batter will have small lumps.)

3. Heat a griddle or skillet over medium-high heat and lightly grease with butter. Scooping batter with a $\frac{1}{4}$-cup (50 mL) measure, pour onto hot griddle or skillet. Sprinkle each pancake with about $\frac{1}{2}$ tbsp (7 mL) of the chocolate chips. Cook until bubbles appear on surface, bottom is golden and edges look firm, about 2 minutes. Flip pancakes and cook until golden, about 1 minute.

Chocolate Chip Pecan Waffles

My children know that it's a special occasion if I'm making waffles for breakfast. I don't know why waffles seem so daunting, because the batter goes together pretty quickly. Maybe it has more to do with where I store my waffle iron, usually in the back of the cupboard behind every other appliance I own.

Tip

To serve these waffles as a dessert, drizzle with maple syrup and top with freshly whipped cream and toasted chopped pecans.

Waffle iron

2 cups	all-purpose flour	500 mL
1/3 cup	chopped pecans	75 mL
1/2 cup	semisweet chocolate chips, coarsely chopped	125 mL
2 tbsp	granulated sugar	25 mL
1 1/2 tsp	baking powder	7 mL
1/2 tsp	baking soda	2 mL
1/4 tsp	salt	1 mL
3	eggs, separated	3
2 cups	buttermilk	500 mL
1 tsp	maple extract or vanilla	5 mL
1/4 cup	unsalted butter, melted and cooled slightly	50 mL
	Vegetable oil	
	Maple syrup	

1. In a medium bowl, combine flour, pecans, chocolate chips, sugar, baking powder, baking soda and salt.

2. In a large bowl, whisk together egg yolks, buttermilk, maple extract and melted butter. Add flour mixture, stirring just until moistened.

3. In a separate bowl, using electric mixer, beat egg whites until soft peaks form. Gently fold egg whites into batter just until there are no streaks. Do not overmix.

4. Heat waffle iron to medium-high and lightly brush with vegetable oil. Scoop about 1/2 cup (125 mL) of the batter onto waffle iron (some waffle irons may take smaller or larger portions). Cook until waffle is crisp and golden brown, about 3 to 5 minutes. Remove from iron. Repeat with remaining batter.

5. Drizzle waffles with maple syrup and serve immediately.

Chocolate Orange French Toast

This is a fun and absolutely delicious breakfast treat. It's like a breakfast sandwich that is stuffed with a chocolate-cinnamon filling. You can add maple syrup if you want, but you might find the French toast is sweet enough without any additional syrup.

Tip

If you are using a narrow loaf of bread, such as a baguette, just increase the number of French toast sandwiches per serving. Depending on the size of bread used, there will probably be some extra batter and filling. Do not use sourdough bread for this recipe.

¾ cup	semisweet chocolate chips	175 mL
¼ cup	unsalted butter	50 mL
2 tbsp	packed light brown sugar	25 mL
1 tbsp	unsweetened Dutch-process cocoa powder	15 mL
¼ tsp	ground cinnamon	1 mL
8	slices French bread, about ½ inch (1 cm) thick (see Tip, left)	8
5	eggs	5
½ cup	orange juice	125 mL
½ cup	milk	125 mL
2 tbsp	orange liqueur	25 mL
1 tsp	vanilla	5 mL
2 tbsp	butter	25 mL
	Warm maple syrup (optional)	
	Orange slices (optional)	

1. In a food processor fitted with a metal blade, mix together chocolate chips, butter, brown sugar, cocoa powder and cinnamon. Process until blended but still somewhat chunky.

2. Spread mixture on 4 of the bread slices. Top with remaining slices.

3. In a large bowl, whisk eggs. Add orange juice, milk, orange liqueur and vanilla. Whisk well. Carefully dip each sandwich in egg mixture, turning to coat each side well.

4. In a large skillet over medium heat, melt butter. Carefully place dipped sandwiches in skillet and cook until browned and crisp on both sides, about 3 to 5 minutes. If sandwiches start to slide apart, gently press down on tops with spatula.

5. Serve French toast with warm maple syrup and fresh orange slices, if desired.

Chocolate-Stuffed Scones

*The stuffing for this scone
recipe was inspired by
Marcy Goldman's chocolate
babka in her book* A Treasury
of Jewish Holiday Baking.
*I thought that my scones
could use a chocolate facelift,
and this marvelous chocolate
filling fits the bill.*

Tip

One scant cup (250 mL)
means just barely that amount,
i.e., just slightly under.

Preheat oven to 425°F (220°C)
Baking sheet, lined with parchment paper

Chocolate Filling

1/2 cup	semisweet chocolate chips	125 mL
3 tbsp	packed light brown sugar	45 mL
2 tbsp	unsalted butter	25 mL
1 tbsp	unsweetened Dutch-process cocoa powder	15 mL
1/2 tsp	ground cinnamon	2 mL

Dough

3 cups	all-purpose flour	750 mL
1/2 cup	granulated sugar	125 mL
2 1/2 tsp	baking powder	12 mL
1/2 tsp	baking soda	2 mL
1/8 tsp	salt	0.5 mL
3/4 cup	unsalted butter, chilled and cut into pieces	175 mL
1 scant cup	buttermilk (see Tip, left)	250 mL

Topping

1 tbsp	granulated sugar	15 mL
1/4 tsp	ground cinnamon	1 mL
1 tbsp	whipping (35%) cream	15 mL

1. *Chocolate Filling:* In a food processor fitted with a metal blade, combine chocolate chips, brown sugar, butter, cocoa powder and cinnamon. Pulse until mixture is blended. Transfer chocolate mixture to a dish and wipe out food processor.

2. *Dough:* In clean food processor fitted with a metal blade, combine flour, sugar, baking powder, baking soda and salt. Pulse for 5 seconds. Add butter and pulse until mixture resembles coarse meal. Add buttermilk and pulse just until dough starts to form a ball.

3. With lightly floured hands, roll dough into 16 equal balls. Place 8 balls on prepared baking sheet, at least 3 inches (7.5 cm) apart. Flatten slightly with your fingers or the heel of your hand. Spoon a heaping tablespoonful (15 mL) of filling in the center of each scone. Place one of remaining balls on top of each and press down lightly to flatten top.

4. *Topping:* In a small bowl, mix together sugar and cinnamon. Brush tops of scones with cream and sprinkle with cinnamon-sugar topping. Bake in preheated oven for about 20 minutes or until crusty and golden brown. Transfer scones to a rack to cool slightly. Serve warm.

Maple-Glazed Chocolate Walnut Breakfast Biscuits

I love the flavor combination of maple, walnuts and chocolate chips. These breakfast biscuits are my favorite way to start the day.

Tips

This recipe can be doubled.

The biscuits are best served the day they are made.

The biscuits can also be patted out and cut into hearts or circles with biscuit or cookie cutters.

Preheat oven to 400°F (200°C)
Baking sheet, lined with parchment paper

2½ cups	all-purpose flour	550 mL
⅓ cup	coarsely chopped walnuts	75 mL
⅓ cup	semisweet chocolate chips	75 mL
¼ cup	granulated sugar	50 mL
1 tbsp	baking powder	15 mL
¼ tsp	salt	1 mL
1¼ cups	whipping (35%) cream	300 mL

Topping (optional)

2 tbsp	whipping (35%) cream	25 mL

Glaze

¾ cup	confectioner's (icing) sugar, sifted	175 mL
4 tsp	milk	20 mL
¼ tsp	maple extract	1 mL

1. In a large bowl, mix together flour, walnuts, chocolate chips, sugar, baking powder and salt. Stir cream into flour mixture just until dough is soft and ragged (see Tips, page 31).

2. Turn out dough onto a lightly floured work surface and gently shape into an 8-inch (20 cm) circle. Using a sharp knife, cut circle into 8 wedges. Transfer wedges to prepared baking sheet, making sure they do not touch or overlap.

3. *Topping:* Lightly brush tops with cream. Bake in preheated oven for 19 minutes or until crisp and golden brown. Transfer biscuits to a rack to cool.

4. *Glaze:* In a medium bowl, whisk together confectioner's sugar, milk and maple extract until smooth. Dip tops of cooled biscuits in glaze. Let biscuits stand on a rack until glaze hardens.

Raspberry Dutch Baby with Chocolate Chips

Serves 4

When I was growing up, Dutch Babies were always a special breakfast treat in our house. This is my mother's original Dutch Baby recipe, which I have updated with raspberries and chocolate chips. I think that she'll approve.

Tip

No matter how tempted you might be not to use the blender, it really makes a big difference in the final product. The blender whips more volume into the eggs than you can by hand. Also, it is important to follow the directions exactly; the Dutch Baby will not rise properly if you blend everything together at once.

Variation

You can substitute cranberries or cherries for the raspberries.

Preheat oven to 425°F (220°C)
9- or 10-inch (23 or 25 cm) deep-dish glass pie plate

1 tbsp	unsalted butter	15 mL
3	eggs	3
¾ cup	milk	175 mL
¾ cup	all-purpose flour	175 mL
½ cup	fresh or frozen raspberries	125 mL
⅓ cup	semisweet chocolate chips	75 mL
	Confectioner's (icing) sugar, for garnish	

1. Place butter in glass dish and set in preheated oven.

2. In a blender, beat eggs on high speed for 1 minute. With motor running, gradually pour in milk, then slowly add flour. Continue blending for 30 seconds.

3. Remove dish from oven and pour batter over hot, melted butter. Sprinkle with raspberries and chocolate chips.

4. Bake in preheated oven for 20 to 22 minutes or until puffed and golden brown. Dust with confectioner's sugar and serve immediately.

Warm Raspberry Chocolate Chip Spread

Here's a new way to enjoy jam, with the addition of melted chocolate. Try this spread warm on everything from scones and toast to pancakes and waffles. You'll wonder why no one has thought of this before.

Tip

When chilled, this spread will get thick and fudge-like (it's delicious eaten right from the spoon). It is divine this way as well, but feel free to warm it slightly in the microwave until spreadable. Just be careful not to reheat for too long or the chocolate could burn.

| ½ cup | raspberry jam (with or without seeds) | 125 mL |
| ½ cup | semisweet chocolate chips | 125 mL |

1. In a microwave-safe bowl, combine jam and chocolate chips. Microwave on High for 2 minutes, stirring every 30 seconds, until jam is warm and chocolate is shiny and almost melted. Stir until smooth.

2. Let cool for 10 minutes. (The mixture will thicken as it cools.)

Cakes

Chocolate-Drizzled Almond Cake

This almond cake has a dense, spongy texture. Freshly whipped cream and strawberries are the perfect accompaniment.

Preheat oven to 350°F (180°C)
8-inch (20 cm) round cake pan,
lined with parchment or waxed paper, greased

1 cup	granulated sugar	250 mL
½ cup	unsalted butter, at room temperature	125 mL
7 oz	almond paste	210 g
1½ tsp	almond extract	7 mL
5	eggs	5
1 cup	all-purpose flour	250 mL
½ tsp	baking powder	2 mL
¼ tsp	salt	1 mL
½ cup	semisweet chocolate chips	125 mL
½ tbsp	shortening	7 mL
	Fresh strawberries (optional)	
	Whipped cream (optional)	

1. In a food processor fitted with a metal blade, combine sugar, butter, almond paste and almond extract. Process until smooth. Add eggs, one at a time, processing well after each addition.

2. In a bowl, sift together flour, baking powder and salt. Add to almond mixture and process just until blended. Pour into prepared pan, smoothing top. Bake in preheated oven for 55 to 60 minutes or until a tester inserted into center comes out clean. Let cake cool in pan on a rack. Run a knife around the side to loosen and invert cake onto a serving plate. Remove parchment.

3. In a microwave-safe bowl, combine chocolate chips and shortening. Microwave on High for 2 minutes, stirring every 30 seconds, until chocolate is shiny and almost melted. Stir until smooth. Using a fork, randomly drizzle the melted chocolate over top of cake. Refrigerate cake until chocolate hardens.

4. Serve cake with fresh strawberries and whipped cream, if desired.

Banana Chocolate Chip Cake

This is not only the ultimate banana bread but also the perfect vehicle for overripe bananas. It is based on a recipe that my mom used to make when my brother and I were growing up. I thought that chocolate chips were needed in an otherwise perfect cake. This cake freezes beautifully, so eat one now and freeze one to enjoy later.

Tip

You can easily freeze overripe bananas, skin and all. Just be sure to thaw them before mashing.

Preheat oven to 350°F (180°C)
Two 9-by 5-inch (2 L) metal loaf pans,
lined with parchment or waxed paper, greased

$2\frac{1}{2}$ cups	all-purpose flour	625 mL
2 tsp	baking soda	10 mL
$\frac{1}{4}$ tsp	salt	1 mL
1 cup	canola oil	250 mL
2 cups	granulated sugar	500 mL
4	eggs	4
2 cups	mashed ripe bananas (about 4 large)	500 mL
1 tsp	vanilla	5 mL
$1\frac{1}{3}$ cups	semisweet chocolate chips	325 mL
$\frac{3}{4}$ cup	toasted walnuts (optional) (see Tip, page 81)	175 mL

1. In a bowl, combine flour, baking soda and salt.

2. In a large bowl, using electric mixer, beat oil and sugar. Add eggs, one at a time, beating well after each addition. Add bananas and vanilla, beating well. Add flour mixture, beating just until smooth. Stir in chocolate chips and walnuts, if using.

3. Spread batter in prepared pans. Bake in preheated oven for 60 to 65 minutes or until a tester inserted into center of cakes comes out clean. Let cakes cool in pans on racks for 15 minutes. Remove from pans and let cool completely on racks.

Chocolate Espresso Lava Cake

Serves 6

I developed this recipe for Bon Appetit Magazine. It was such a huge hit that it was prepared on the "Today Show." These cakes are really chocolate brownie soufflés that are baked in coffee mugs. They are truly delicious, embodying everything that a chocolate dessert should be. You can make them ahead of time, then pop them in the oven as your guests sit down for the main course.

Six 1-cup (250 mL) ovenproof ceramic coffee mugs, greased

1 cup	all-purpose flour	250 mL
3/4 cup	unsweetened Dutch-process cocoa powder	175 mL
5 tsp	instant espresso powder	25 mL
1 1/2 tsp	baking powder	7 mL
1 cup	butter, melted	250 mL
1 cup	granulated sugar	250 mL
1 cup	packed light brown sugar	250 mL
4	eggs	4
1 1/2 tsp	vanilla	7 mL
1/4 tsp	almond extract	1 mL
3/4 cup	semisweet chocolate chips	175 mL

Topping

1 cup	whipping (35%) cream, chilled	250 mL
3 tbsp	confectioner's (icing) sugar	45 mL
1 tsp	instant espresso powder	5 mL

1. In a medium bowl, sift together flour, cocoa powder, espresso powder and baking powder.

2. In a large bowl, whisk together melted butter and granulated and brown sugars until well blended. Whisk in eggs, one at a time, then vanilla and almond extract. Whisk in flour mixture. Divide batter among prepared coffee mugs (about 2/3 cup/150 mL in each). Top each with 2 tbsp (25 mL) of the chocolate chips. Gently press chips into batter. Cover and refrigerate mugs for at least 1 hour or for up to 1 day.

3. *Topping:* In a medium bowl, combine cream, confectioner's sugar and espresso powder. Whisk until stiff peaks form. Chill for 1 hour.

4. Preheat oven to 350°F (180°C). Let mugs with batter stand at room temperature for 5 minutes. Bake, uncovered, until cakes are puffed and crusty and tester inserted into center comes out with thick batter attached, about 30 minutes. Let cool in mugs on a rack for 5 minutes. Top hot cakes with espresso whipped cream and serve.

Chocolate Chip Calypso Cake

Chocolate and ginger are a magical combination, transforming an otherwise plain cake into something extraordinary. This cake is divine with a cup of hot tea, preferably Earl Grey.

Tip

To make hot brewed Earl Grey tea, combine 1¼ cups (300 mL) boiling water with 2 Earl Grey tea bags in a glass measuring cup. Let stand for 5 minutes before using.

Variation

Substitute boiling water for the tea.

Preheat oven to 350°F (180°C)
13-by 9-inch (3 L) metal baking pan, lined with parchment or waxed paper, greased

2½ cups	all-purpose flour	625 mL
1 tbsp	ground ginger	15 mL
2 tsp	baking soda	10 mL
1 tsp	ground cinnamon	5 mL
½ tsp	baking powder	2 mL
½ tsp	ground allspice	2 mL
¼ tsp	ground nutmeg	1 mL
¼ tsp	salt	1 mL
¾ cup	unsalted butter, melted and cooled	175 mL
¾ cup	granulated sugar	175 mL
¾ cup	light fancy molasses	175 mL
2	eggs	2
1 cup	hot brewed tea, preferably Earl Grey (see Tip, left)	250 mL
⅓ cup	chopped crystallized ginger	75 mL
¾ cup	semisweet chocolate chips	175 mL
	Confectioner's (icing) sugar (optional)	

1. In a medium bowl, combine flour, ground ginger, baking soda, cinnamon, baking powder, allspice, nutmeg and salt.

2. In a large bowl, using electric mixer, beat butter and sugar until light and fluffy. Beat in molasses. Add eggs, one at a time, beating well after each addition. Stir in flour mixture alternately with hot tea, making three additions of flour mixture and two of tea, beating just until smooth. Stir in crystallized ginger.

3. Spread batter in prepared pan. Sprinkle top evenly with chocolate chips. Bake in preheated oven for 30 minutes or until a tester inserted into center comes out clean. Let cake cool in pan on rack.

4. Serve lightly dusted with confectioner's sugar, if desired.

Chocolate Midnight

This flourless cake is a delectable blend of dark chocolate and espresso. Serve slices with a scoop of premium vanilla ice cream.

Tip

To remove cake from springform pan, run a knife around edge of pan to loosen. Remove side of pan. Invert cake onto platter and remove parchment.

Variation

Omit ground espresso.

Preheat oven to 350°F (180°C)

10-inch (25 cm) springform pan, lined with parchment or waxed paper, greased

1½ cups	semisweet chocolate chips	375 mL
1 cup	unsalted butter	250 mL
1 tbsp	rum	15 mL
1 tsp	vanilla	5 mL
6	eggs	6
1 cup	granulated sugar	250 mL
1 cup	unsweetened Dutch-process cocoa powder, sifted	250 mL
2 tbsp	finely ground espresso	25 mL
¼ tsp	salt	1 mL

1. In a microwave-safe bowl, combine chocolate chips and butter. Microwave on High for 2 minutes, stirring every 30 seconds, until chocolate is shiny and almost melted. Stir until smooth. Whisk in rum and vanilla. Set aside.

2. In a large bowl, whisk eggs. Whisk in sugar, cocoa powder, chocolate mixture, ground espresso and salt just until smooth.

3. Pour mixture into prepared pan and bake in preheated oven, about 55 minutes or until a tester inserted into center comes out clean. Let cool in pan on a rack. Remove from pan (see Tip, left) and serve.

Chocolate Chip Chai Cake

This is a delightful cake filled with the creamy, slightly spicy flavors of chai tea. It's great on its own, but I also thought a caramel frosting would be good, so I developed a brown sugar icing inspired by a recipe by Lee Bailey.

Tips

To substitute loose chai tea, grind it in a coffee or spice grinder until you have little bits (it doesn't have to be finely powdered). For 2 tea bags, substitute 2 tsp (10 mL) ground loose tea.

Leftover cake freezes very well for about 1 month (that is, if you happen to have any left).

Preheat oven to 350°F (180°C)
13-by 9-inch (3 L) metal baking pan, greased

2 cups	all-purpose flour	500 mL
1 tsp	baking powder	5 mL
1/2 tsp	baking soda	2 mL
1/2 tsp	ground cardamom	2 mL
1/4 tsp	ground allspice	1 mL
1/4 tsp	salt	1 mL
2	chai spice tea bags (see Tips, left)	2
1/2 cup	unsalted butter, at room temperature	125 mL
1 3/4 cups	granulated sugar	425 mL
4	egg whites	4
1 tsp	vanilla	5 mL
1 1/3 cups	buttermilk	325 mL
3/4 cup	semisweet chocolate chips	175 mL

Icing (optional)

1 cup	packed brown sugar	250 mL
1/2 cup	whipping (35%) cream	125 mL
1/4 cup	butter	50 mL
2 cups	confectioner's (icing) sugar, sifted	500 mL
1 tsp	vanilla	5 mL

1. In a medium bowl, combine flour, baking powder, baking soda, cardamom, allspice, salt and contents of tea bags.

2. In a large bowl, using electric mixer, beat butter and sugar until light and fluffy. Add egg whites, one at a time, beating well after each addition. Stir in vanilla.

3. Beat flour mixture into butter mixture alternately with buttermilk, making three additions of flour mixture and two of buttermilk. Beat just until smooth. Stir in chocolate chips.

4. Spread batter in prepared pan. Bake in preheated oven for 35 to 40 minutes or until cake is golden brown and pulling away from sides of pan and a tester inserted into center comes out clean. Let cake cool in pan on a rack while preparing icing.

5. *Icing:* In a large saucepan over medium heat, bring brown sugar, cream and butter to a rolling boil. Remove pan from heat and transfer mixture to a mixing bowl. Whisk in confectioner's sugar and vanilla until blended. Using an electric mixer, beat icing until thick and just warm to the touch. Spread over cake. Let cool completely.

Chocolate Cherry Rum Cakes

I have always loved chocolate and cherries together, but then again, who doesn't? One day a thought occurred to me: What would happen if I added these two ingredients to a rum cake batter? The answer lies in this fantastic cake.

Variation

Substitute dried cranberries for the cherries.

Preheat oven to 375°F (190°C)
Four 6-by 3-inch (375 mL) loaf pans,
lined with parchment or waxed paper, greased

2½ cups	all-purpose flour	625 mL
2½ tsp	baking powder	12 mL
¼ tsp	salt	1 mL
⅔ cup	unsalted butter, at room temperature	150 mL
1¾ cups	granulated sugar	425 mL
2	eggs	2
1 tsp	vanilla	5 mL
¾ cup	milk	175 mL
½ cup	light rum	125 mL
⅔ cup	semisweet chocolate chips	150 mL
⅔ cup	dried sour cherries	150 mL

Glaze

¾ cup	granulated sugar	175 mL
½ cup	unsalted butter	125 mL
¼ cup	light rum	50 mL
¼ cup	water	50 mL

1. In a medium bowl, combine flour, baking powder and salt.

2. In a large bowl, using electric mixer, beat butter and sugar. Add eggs, one at a time, beating well after each addition. Beat in vanilla. Add flour mixture to butter mixture alternately with milk, making three additions of flour mixture and two of milk. Add rum, beating just until smooth. Stir in chocolate chips and cherries.

3. Divide batter among prepared pans. Bake in preheated oven for 36 to 38 minutes or until a tester inserted into center of cakes comes out clean. Remove cakes from oven and, using a skewer or toothpick, poke holes randomly over tops.

4. *Glaze:* Meanwhile, in a large saucepan over medium heat, combine sugar, butter, rum and water. Let simmer for 3 to 4 minutes, until sugar is dissolved. Remove from heat. Spoon glaze over tops of hot cakes. Use most of glaze, even if it takes several applications.

5. Let cakes cool in pans on racks for 30 minutes. Remove cakes from pans and invert onto racks. Drizzle with remaining glaze. Let cool completely on racks.

Chocolate Mousse-Filled Cupcakes

These cupcakes are a grown-up version of the store-bought treats beloved by children. Devil's food cupcakes are filled with a luscious chocolate mousse center and topped with a coating of chocolate ganache.

Tip

The cupcakes will keep for up to 1 day, but they are best eaten the day they are made.

Preheat oven to 350°F (180°C)
Two muffin pans, greased or lined with paper liners
Baking sheet, lined with foil or parchment paper

1½ cups	all-purpose flour	375 mL
¾ cup	unsweetened Dutch-process cocoa powder	175 mL
1 tsp	baking soda	5 mL
1 tsp	baking powder	5 mL
¼ tsp	salt	1 mL
2	eggs	2
1¾ cups	granulated sugar	425 mL
½ cup	vegetable oil	125 mL
1 tsp	vanilla	5 mL
1¼ cups	strong brewed coffee, at room temperature	300 mL

Filling

⅓ cup	semisweet chocolate chips	75 mL
1 tbsp	strong brewed coffee	15 mL
¾ cup	whipping (35%) cream	175 mL
1 tbsp	confectioner's (icing) sugar	15 mL

Glaze

⅔ cup	whipping (35%) cream	150 mL
1 cup	semisweet chocolate chips	250 mL

1. In a medium bowl, sift together flour, cocoa powder, baking soda, baking powder and salt.

2. In a large bowl, using electric mixer, beat eggs, sugar, oil and vanilla until creamy. Add flour mixture, beating just until combined. Beat in coffee until smooth. Do not overbeat.

3. Fill prepared muffin cups with batter. Bake in preheated oven for 22 to 24 minutes, until cupcakes are just firm to the touch and a tester inserted into center of cupcake comes out clean. Let cool in pans on racks for 10 minutes. Remove from pans and let cool completely on racks.

4. *Filling:* In a microwave-safe dish, combine chocolate chips and coffee. Microwave on High for $2\frac{1}{2}$ minutes, stirring every 30 seconds, until chocolate is shiny and almost melted. Stir until smooth. Remove from microwave and stir until chocolate is melted and smooth. Let cool slightly.

5. In a large bowl, using electric mixer, whip cream and confectioner's sugar until almost stiff peaks. Add melted chocolate mixture, beating just until incorporated. Finish mixing by hand with a rubber spatula.

6. Using a sharp paring knife, gently cut a $\frac{3}{4}$-inch (2 cm) cone from the bottom of each cupcake and trim point off cone. Using a small spoon, fill each hole with chocolate cream filling and replace reserved cones. Place on prepared baking sheet and refrigerate while preparing glaze.

7. *Glaze:* In a microwave-safe bowl, microwave cream on High until it starts to simmer, about 40 seconds. Add chocolate chips and whisk until melted and shiny. Stir until smooth. Set aside to cool for 10 minutes. Dip tops of each filled cupcake in chocolate glaze. Place dipped cupcakes on prepared baking sheet and refrigerate until ready to serve.

Coconut Chocolate Chip Bundt Cake

This name is fun to repeat over and over. It is equally fun to enjoy the combination of chocolate and coconut time and time again. To "gild the lily," I've combined them in one cake.

Preheat oven to 325°F (160°C)

10-inch (3 L) Bundt pan, greased and floured

3 cups	all-purpose flour	750 mL
1/2 tsp	baking soda	2 mL
1/4 tsp	salt	1 mL
1 cup	unsalted butter, at room temperature	250 mL
2 cups	granulated sugar	500 mL
1	package (8 oz/250 g) cream cheese, softened	1
3	eggs	3
1 tsp	vanilla	5 mL
1/2 cup	unsweetened coconut milk	125 mL
3/4 cup	buttermilk	175 mL
1 cup	lightly packed sweetened flaked coconut	250 mL
3/4 cup	semisweet chocolate chips	175 mL

Icing

1 cup	confectioner's (icing) sugar, sifted	250 mL
1 1/2 tbsp	milk	22 mL
1/2 tsp	rum	2 mL
1/2 cup	sweetened flaked coconut, toasted (see Tip, page 62)	125 mL

1. In a bowl, combine flour, baking soda and salt.

2. In a large bowl, using electric mixer, beat butter and sugar until light and fluffy. Beat in cream cheese until smooth. Add eggs, one at a time, beating well after each addition. Add vanilla, beating well. Combine coconut milk and buttermilk. Mix in flour mixture alternately with coconut milk-buttermilk mixture, making three additions of flour mixture and two of milk mixture, just until smooth. Stir in chocolate chips.

3. Spread batter in prepared pan, smoothing top. Bake in preheated oven for 65 to 80 minutes or until a tester inserted into center of cake comes out clean and cake starts to pull away from sides of pan. Let cake cool in pan on a rack for 15 minutes. Carefully invert cake onto a large plate. Let cool completely.

4. *Icing:* Meanwhile, whisk together confectioner's sugar, milk and rum until smooth. Set aside until cake is cool. Whisk again before drizzling or spooning over top of cake. Sprinkle with toasted coconut.

Chocolate Mousse Cake

Although this seems like a very labor-intensive cake, it really isn't. In fact, it can be made a day ahead, making it a perfect do-ahead dessert. Plus, as an added bonus, it freezes beautifully.

Tip

You can garnish cake with a sprinkling of chocolate chips or sprinkle it with pieces of broken sandwich cookies.

Variation

Substitute another liqueur for the Kirsch (cherry brandy), such as Irish Cream, crème de cacao or crème de menthe.

10-inch (25 cm) springform pan, greased

36	cream-filled chocolate sandwich cookies	36
¼ cup	unsalted butter, melted	50 mL
Filling		
2¾ cups	semisweet chocolate chips	675 mL
4 cups	whipping (35%) cream, chilled and divided	1 L
1 tbsp	Kirsch or other liqueur (see Variation, left)	15 mL
Topping		
1 cup	whipping (35%) cream, chilled	250 mL
3 tbsp	confectioner's (icing) sugar	45 mL
½ tsp	vanilla	2 mL

1. In a food processor fitted with a metal blade, pulse chocolate sandwich cookies until finely ground. (You should have about 3 cups/750 mL.) Add melted butter and process just until combined. Firmly press cookie mixture onto bottom and up side of prepared pan. Freeze for 20 minutes to firm up crust.

2. *Filling:* Meanwhile, in a large microwave-safe bowl, combine chocolate chips and 1 cup (250 mL) of the cream. Microwave on High for 2½ minutes, stirring every 30 seconds, until chocolate is shiny and almost melted. Stir until smooth. In clean food processor bowl, process chocolate mixture and Kirsch until smooth.

3. In a large bowl, whip remaining cream until stiff peaks form. Add cooled chocolate mixture and whip until incorporated. Spread filling over prepared crust and refrigerate until firm, about 6 hours, or overnight.

4. *Topping:* Whip cream with confectioner's sugar and vanilla until stiff peaks form. Spread over chocolate mousse layer and refrigerate for 1 hour or until firm, or freeze for 20 minutes. Carefully run a knife around edge of pan before removing side. Do not remove bottom of pan. Slice and serve cake directly from bottom of pan.

Chocolate Port Torte

Do you like grown-up desserts that can be assembled in a jiffy and, above all else, taste fantastic? Then this one's for you! One of my husband's favorites, it has a truffle-like texture with the deep flavors of dark chocolate and port wine.

Tips

Don't be daunted by the water bath. It is actually a very simple technique to ensure a smooth-textured cake.

Dust with unsweetened cocoa powder or confectioner's sugar.

Preheat oven to 350°F (180°C)

10-inch (25 cm) round cake pan, lined with parchment or waxed paper, greased

Roasting pan large enough to hold cake pan for water bath

2½ cups	semisweet chocolate chips	625 mL
2 cups	unsalted butter	500 mL
3 oz	unsweetened chocolate, chopped	90 g
2 cups	granulated sugar	500 mL
1 cup	port wine	250 mL
⅛ tsp	salt	0.5 mL
8	eggs	8

1. In a large microwave-safe bowl, combine chocolate chips, butter and unsweetened chocolate. Microwave on High for 2 minutes, stirring every 30 seconds, until chocolate is shiny and almost melted. Stir until smooth. Whisk in sugar, port wine and salt.

2. In a large bowl, whisk eggs until blended. Add melted chocolate mixture, whisking until smooth. Pour chocolate mixture into prepared cake pan.

3. Place pan in a roasting pan in preheated oven. Pour in enough warm water to come 1 inch (2.5 cm) up side of cake pan. Bake for 70 to 75 minutes or until top of cake has risen, feels firm and crisp to the touch and a knife inserted into center comes out almost clean (it will look a little moist). Do not overbake.

4. Transfer pan with water bath to a cooling rack. Let stand for 20 minutes. Remove cake from water bath and let cool completely on rack. Refrigerate until firm. To serve, invert cake onto a serving platter. Remove parchment paper.

Coconut Cupcakes

Makes 12 cupcakes

These cupcakes have been my brother Jon's favorite for years. The scrumptious chocolate chip cake, creamy icing and toasted coconut make them a winner.

Tip

A great way to toast coconut is in a nonstick skillet. Heat coconut in skillet over medium-high heat, stirring constantly. Cook, stirring, just until coconut starts to turn light golden brown, about 3 minutes. Be careful not to burn. Transfer to a plate and let cool.

Preheat oven to 350°F (180°C)
Muffin pan, lined with paper liners or greased

1 cup	all-purpose flour	250 mL
1/2 tsp	baking powder	2 mL
1/4 tsp	baking soda	1 mL
1/8 tsp	salt	0.5 mL
1/4 cup	unsalted butter, at room temperature	50 mL
3/4 cup	granulated sugar	175 mL
1/2 tsp	vanilla	2 mL
2	egg whites	2
2/3 cup	buttermilk	150 mL
1/2 cup	semisweet chocolate chips	125 mL

Icing

6 oz	cream cheese, softened	175 g
1/2 cup	unsalted butter	125 mL
1 tsp	vanilla	5 mL
1/4 tsp	almond extract	1 mL
2 3/4 cups	confectioner's (icing) sugar, sifted	675 mL
1/2 cup	whipping (35%) cream	125 mL
3/4 cup	sweetened flaked coconut, lightly toasted (see Tip, left)	175 mL

1. In a small bowl, combine flour, baking powder, baking soda and salt.

2. In a large bowl, using electric mixer, beat butter and sugar until light and fluffy. Beat in vanilla. Add egg whites, one at a time, beating well after each addition. Alternately beat in flour mixture and buttermilk on low speed, making three additions of flour mixture and two of buttermilk, just until combined. Stir in chocolate chips.

3. Divide batter among prepared muffin cups, filling each halfway. Bake in preheated oven for about 25 minutes or until a tester inserted into center comes out clean. Let cool in pan on a rack for 5 minutes. Remove from pan and let cool completely on rack.

4. *Icing:* Meanwhile, beat cream cheese, butter, vanilla and almond extract until fluffy. Gradually beat in confectioner's sugar until light and fluffy. Add cream, beating until incorporated. With mixer on high speed, beat icing until it is whipped, fluffy and forms soft peaks.

5. Spread icing on cooled cupcakes. Generously sprinkle toasted coconut over icing.

Chocolate Chip Cream Cheese Pound Cake

This is the best pound cake you will ever taste. It is very quick to make and disappears just as quickly. Exercise patience while waiting for it to bake. It will keep, wrapped, for several days.

Tip

Because this recipe makes two cakes, go ahead and freeze one so that you have something on hand for unexpected company.

Variation

Substitute 2 tsp (10 mL) almond extract for the vanilla.

Preheat oven to 325°F (160°C)
Two 9-by 5-inch (2 L) metal loaf pans,
lined with parchment or waxed paper, greased

3 cups	all-purpose flour	750 mL
1/4 tsp	salt	1 mL
1 1/2 cups	unsalted butter, at room temperature	375 mL
1	package (8 oz/250 g) cream cheese, softened	1
3 cups	granulated sugar	750 mL
6	eggs	6
1 1/2 tsp	vanilla	7 mL
1 1/2 cups	semisweet chocolate chips	375 mL

1. In a medium bowl, combine flour and salt.

2. In a large bowl, using electric mixer, beat butter, cream cheese and sugar until light and fluffy. Add eggs, one at a time, beating well after each addition. Add flour mixture and vanilla, beating just until smooth. Stir in chocolate chips.

3. Spread batter in prepared pans. Bake in preheated oven for 1 1/2 hours to 1 hour and 40 minutes or until golden and a tester inserted into center comes out clean. Let cakes cool in pans for 15 minutes. Carefully invert cakes onto racks (the cakes can break apart easily). Let cool completely on racks. Peel off parchment.

Chocolate Mousse-Filled Cupcakes *(page 56)*

Overleaf: Little Chocolate Cakes *(page 74)* and Chocolate-Drizzled Almond Cake *(page 46)*

Double Chocolate Zucchini Cake

This cake has been a favorite over the years. Unless you mention it, no one would guess that there is zucchini in it. The shredded zucchini provides incredible moisture, while the cocoa and chocolate chips provide the fudge flavor.

Tip

This cake freezes very well for up to 2 months, so if you find yourself with a bumper crop of zucchini, be sure to make this cake.

Preheat oven to 350°F (180°C)
Two 9-by 5-inch (2 L) metal loaf pans,
lined with parchment or waxed paper, greased

2 cups	all-purpose flour	500 mL
1/2 cup	unsweetened Dutch-process cocoa powder, sifted	125 mL
1 tsp	baking soda	5 mL
1 tsp	baking powder	5 mL
1 tsp	ground cinnamon	5 mL
1/2 tsp	ground nutmeg	2 mL
1/2 tsp	ground allspice	2 mL
1/4 tsp	salt	1 mL
1 cup	vegetable oil	250 mL
2 cups	granulated sugar	500 mL
4	eggs	4
1 tsp	vanilla	5 mL
3 cups	lightly packed shredded zucchini (about 3 zucchini)	750 mL
1 cup	semisweet chocolate chips	250 mL

1. In a medium bowl, combine flour, cocoa powder, baking soda, baking powder, cinnamon, nutmeg, allspice and salt.

2. In a large bowl, using electric mixer, beat oil and sugar. Add eggs, one at a time, beating well after each addition. Beat in vanilla. Add flour mixture, beating just until smooth. Stir in zucchini and chocolate chips.

3. Spread batter in prepared pans. Bake in preheated oven for 1 hour or until a tester inserted into center comes out clean. Let cakes cool in pans on racks for 15 minutes. Remove parchment.

Chocolate Mousse Cake *(page 60)*

Cranberry Sour Cream Bundt Cake

Serves 12

My daughter suggested I mention that this is a very grown-up cake. As I was developing this recipe, I decided to send the cake with her to her sixth grade class. The teachers demolished the cake in mere minutes, while the kids waited patiently for chocolate chip cookies. Go figure.

Tip

Although this cake is delicious the day it is made, the flavors and textures are even better the next day.

Preheat oven to 325°F (160°C)
10-inch (3 L) Bundt pan, greased and floured

3 cups	all-purpose flour	750 mL
1/2 tsp	baking powder	2 mL
1/4 tsp	baking soda	1 mL
1/4 tsp	salt	1 mL
1 cup	unsalted butter, at room temperature	250 mL
2 cups	granulated sugar	500 mL
1 cup	sour cream	250 mL
6	eggs	6
2 tbsp	orange liqueur	25 mL
1 tbsp	grated orange zest	15 mL
1 tsp	vanilla	5 mL
1 1/3 cups	fresh or frozen cranberries	325 mL
3/4 cup	semisweet chocolate chips	175 mL

Icing

1 cup	confectioner's (icing) sugar, sifted	250 mL
1 1/2 tbsp	freshly squeezed orange juice (approx.)	22 mL
	Confectioner's sugar, for dusting (optional)	

1. In a medium bowl, combine flour, baking powder, baking soda and salt.

2. In a large bowl, using electric mixer, beat butter and sugar until light and fluffy. Beat in sour cream. Add eggs, one at a time, beating well after each addition. Add orange liqueur, orange zest and vanilla. Add flour mixture, beating just until smooth. Fold in cranberries and chocolate chips.

3. Spread batter in prepared pan. Bake in preheated oven for 75 to 80 minutes or until a tester inserted into center of cake comes out clean. Let cake cool in pan on a rack for 15 minutes. Carefully invert cake onto a large plate. Let cool completely.

4. *Icing:* Meanwhile, whisk together confectioner's sugar and orange juice until smooth, adding up to 1 tsp (5 mL) more juice if necessary for desired consistency. Set aside until cake is cool. Whisk again before drizzling or pouring over top of cake. When icing hardens, transfer cake to a serving platter. Lightly dust with confectioner's sugar, if desired.

Eggnog Chocolate Chip Tea Cake

This cake has all of the flavors of Christmas. You can usually find eggnog in the grocery store from October through January.

Variation

You can garnish this cake with a light dusting of confectioner's sugar or you can drizzle it with an eggnog glaze. To make a glaze, simply whisk together 2 cups (500 mL) confectioner's (icing) sugar, sifted, 3 tbsp (45 mL) eggnog and 1 tsp (5 mL) rum. Drizzle over cake.

Preheat oven to 350°F (180°C)
9-by 5-inch (2 L) metal loaf pan,
lined with parchment or waxed paper, greased

3 cups	all-purpose flour	750 mL
1 tbsp	baking powder	15 mL
1½ tsp	ground nutmeg	7 mL
½ cup	unsalted butter, at room temperature	125 mL
¾ cup	granulated sugar	175 mL
2	eggs	2
1¾ cups	eggnog	425 mL
¼ cup	dark rum	50 mL
½ cup	semisweet chocolate chips	125 mL

1. In a medium bowl, combine flour, baking powder and nutmeg.

2. In a large bowl, using electric mixer, beat butter and sugar until light and fluffy. Add eggs, one at a time, beating well after each addition. Add eggnog and rum, beating well. Add flour mixture, beating just until combined. Fold in chocolate chips.

3. Spread batter in prepared pan. Bake in preheated oven for 70 minutes or until cake is golden and a tester inserted into center comes out clean.

4. Let cake cool in pan on rack for 15 minutes. Remove parchment.

Mocha Chocolate Chip Cake

For years, people have begged me to share this loaf cake recipe. This has been a closely guarded secret — until now. It is pure nirvana for coffee lovers.

Preheat oven to 350°F (180°C)
9-by 5-inch (2 L) metal loaf pan, lined with parchment or waxed paper, greased

1/2 cup	hot strong brewed coffee	125 mL
1/4 cup	finely ground coffee	50 mL
2 tbsp	instant coffee granules	25 mL
2 cups	all-purpose flour	500 mL
2 tsp	baking powder	10 mL
2 tsp	ground cinnamon	10 mL
1/4 tsp	salt	1 mL
1 cup	vegetable oil	250 mL
1 3/4 cups	granulated sugar	425 mL
3	eggs	3
2 tsp	vanilla	10 mL
1/2 cup	semisweet chocolate chips	125 mL

1. In a bowl, combine brewed coffee and finely ground and instant coffee, stirring well. Set aside to cool.

2. In a medium bowl, combine flour, baking powder, cinnamon and salt.

3. In a large bowl, using electric mixer, beat oil, sugar and eggs until smooth. Add cooled coffee mixture and vanilla, beating well. Add flour mixture and beat on medium-high speed for 10 seconds, just until blended.

4. Pour batter into prepared pan. Sprinkle chocolate chips over top, lightly pressing some of the chips into batter. Bake in preheated oven for 65 to 70 minutes or until a tester inserted into center of cake comes out clean.

5. Let cool in pan on rack for 15 minutes. Remove cake from pan and let cool completely on rack.

Rich Lemon
Chocolate Chip Bundt Cake

Sometimes strange bedfellows make the best relationships. Take chocolate and lemon, for example. This is a dynamite combination, one that often catches people by surprise — and a pleasant one at that. You can make this cake ahead of time as it is good for several days.

Tips

This cake needs to be made in a stand mixer; otherwise, the cream cheese separates from the batter during baking.

Do not freeze this cake or it will become very rubbery.

Preheat oven to 350°F (180°C)
Electric stand mixer
10-inch (3 L) Bundt pan, greased and floured

3 cups	all-purpose flour	750 mL
1/2 tsp	baking soda	2 mL
1/4 tsp	salt	1 mL
1 cup	unsalted butter, at room temperature	250 mL
2 cups	granulated sugar	500 mL
1	package (8 oz/250 g) cream cheese, softened	1
3	eggs	3
1 tsp	lemon extract	5 mL
1 tbsp	grated lemon zest	15 mL
2 tbsp	freshly squeezed lemon juice	25 mL
1 cup	buttermilk	250 mL
1 cup	semisweet chocolate chips	250 mL

Icing

1 cup	confectioner's (icing) sugar, sifted	250 mL
1 1/2 tbsp	freshly squeezed lemon juice (approx.)	22 mL

1. In a small bowl, combine flour, baking soda and salt.

2. In a large bowl, using electric mixer, beat butter and sugar until light and fluffy. Add cream cheese, beating until smooth. Add eggs, one at a time, beating well after each addition. Add lemon extract, lemon zest and lemon juice, beating well. Mix in flour mixture alternately with buttermilk, making three additions of flour mixture and two of buttermilk, just until smooth. Stir in chocolate chips.

3. Spread batter in prepared pan, smoothing top. Bake in preheated oven for about 70 minutes or until a tester inserted into center of cake comes out clean and cake starts to pull away from sides of pan. Let cake cool in pan on a rack for 15 minutes. Carefully invert cake onto a large plate. Let cool completely.

4. *Icing:* Meanwhile, whisk together confectioner's sugar and lemon juice until smooth, adding up to 1 tsp (5 mL) more juice if necessary for desired consistency. Set aside until cake is cool. Whisk again before drizzling or pouring over top of cake. When icing hardens, transfer cake to a serving platter.

Lone Star
Double Chocolate Chip Cake

Several years ago, large chocolate sheet cakes called Texas Sheet Cakes (I guess for their big size) were all the rage. I thought that they needed something new, so here is a twist. This rich, dark chocolate cake is studded with chocolate chips and a creamy chocolate coffee icing. One of the great things about this cake (without the icing) is that it contains no dairy or eggs, perfect for vegans or people with allergies.

Tip

A great ratio for strong brewed coffee is 2 tbsp (25 mL) finely ground French roast coffee or espresso for every ¾ cup (175 mL) water.

Variation

To make this cake dairy-free, substitute dairy-free chocolate chips, soy beverage for the milk and margarine for the butter.

Preheat oven to 350°F (180°C)
13-by 9-inch (3 L) metal baking pan, greased

2⅓ cups	all-purpose flour	575 mL
¾ cup	unsweetened Dutch-process cocoa powder	175 mL
1 tsp	baking soda	5 mL
¼ tsp	salt	1 mL
¾ cup	vegetable oil	175 mL
2 cups	granulated sugar	500 mL
1¼ cups	strong brewed coffee, at room temperature	300 mL
1 tsp	vanilla	5 mL
½ tsp	almond extract	2 mL
1½ tbsp	balsamic vinegar	22 mL
1 cup	semisweet chocolate chips	250 mL

Icing

2½ cups	confectioner's (icing) sugar, sifted	625 mL
1½ cups	unsweetened Dutch-process cocoa powder	375 mL
1 cup	unsalted butter or margarine, at room temperature	250 mL
2 tbsp	strong brewed coffee, at room temperature (see Tip, left)	25 mL
2 tsp	vanilla	10 mL
2 tbsp	milk	25 mL
1 tbsp	dark rum	15 mL

1. In a medium bowl, sift together flour, cocoa powder, baking soda and salt.

2. In a large bowl, using electric mixer, beat oil and sugar. Beat in coffee, vanilla and almond extract. Add flour mixture, beating until smooth. Beat in balsamic vinegar just until mixed.

3. Quickly pour batter into prepared pan and sprinkle with chocolate chips. Bake in preheated oven for 50 minutes or until a tester inserted into center of cake comes out clean. Let cake cool completely in pan on rack.

4. *Icing:* Meanwhile, in a food processor fitted with a metal blade, combine confectioner's sugar, cocoa powder, butter, coffee and vanilla. Process until smooth. Add milk and rum. Process until smooth, scraping down side of bowl as necessary. Spread desired amount of icing over cooled cake. Any extra icing can be covered and refrigerated for another use. Bring to room temperature before using.

Little Chocolate Cakes

Serve these elegant little cakes warm so that the center is soft and gooey. I like to make them for special occasions, dressed up with a little raspberry sauce or a scoop of raspberry sorbet.

Tip

These cakes lend themselves nicely to several different garnishes. You can lightly dust with confectioner's (icing) sugar or serve with a scoop of raspberry sorbet.

Variation

Lightly sprinkle cakes with ground cinnamon before serving.

Preheat oven to 350°F (180°C)
Six standard-size ramekins, greased
Baking sheet

¾ cup	semisweet chocolate chips	175 mL
2 oz	unsweetened chocolate, chopped	60 g
⅔ cup	unsalted butter, at room temperature	150 mL
1 tsp	brandy	5 mL
⅛ tsp	salt	0.5 mL
2	eggs	2
4	egg yolks	4
½ cup	granulated sugar	125 mL
2 tbsp	all-purpose flour	25 mL
1 tbsp	unsweetened Dutch-process cocoa powder	15 mL

1. In a medium microwave-safe bowl, combine chocolate chips, unsweetened chocolate and butter. Microwave on High for 2 minutes, stirring every 30 seconds, until chocolate is shiny and almost melted. Stir until smooth. Whisk in brandy and salt. Set aside to cool slightly.

2. In a large bowl, using electric mixer, beat eggs and egg yolks with sugar for 2 to 3 minutes or until thickened, pale and the consistency of soft whipped cream. Fold in half of the chocolate mixture until blended. Fold in remaining chocolate mixture.

3. In a small bowl, combine flour and cocoa powder. Sift over top of batter and gently fold in until incorporated.

4. Divide batter among prepared ramekins and place on baking sheet. Bake in preheated oven for 15 minutes or until tops of cakes are puffed and just starting to crack. Remove from pan and let cool on rack for 3 minutes. Gently run a sharp paring knife around edge of cakes and invert onto serving plates. Serve immediately.

Pumpkin Chocolate Chip Loaves

Pumpkin and spice make this a great quick bread to serve in the fall. It is amazing how well the flavors of pumpkin and chocolate go together.

Tip

These loaves freeze very well for up to 1 month. I like to keep a few on hand for brunch or a last-minute dessert.

Variation

Add 1 cup (250 mL) coarsely chopped walnuts or pecans when you stir in the chocolate chips.

Preheat oven to 350°F (180°C)
Two 9-by 5-inch (3 L) metal loaf pans,
lined with parchment or waxed paper, greased

3 cups	all-purpose flour	750 mL
2 tsp	ground cinnamon	10 mL
1½ tsp	baking powder	7 mL
1½ tsp	baking soda	7 mL
1 tsp	ground allspice	5 mL
1 tsp	ground nutmeg	5 mL
½ tsp	salt	2 mL
1 cup	vegetable oil	250 mL
3 cups	granulated sugar	750 mL
4	eggs	4
2 cups	canned pumpkin purée (not pie filling)	500 mL
¼ cup	water	50 mL
1⅓ cups	semisweet chocolate chips	325 mL

1. In a medium bowl, combine flour, cinnamon, baking powder, baking soda, allspice, nutmeg and salt.

2. In a large bowl, using electric mixer, beat oil and sugar. Beat in eggs, one at a time, beating well after each addition. Beat in pumpkin and water. Stir in flour mixture just until smooth. Stir in chocolate chips.

3. Spread batter in prepared pans. Bake in preheated oven for for 70 minutes or until a tester inserted into center comes out clean. Let cakes cool in pans on rack for 10 minutes. Run a sharp knife around edge of loaves and remove from pan. Place loaves on racks and let cool completely. Remove parchment.

Sour Cream Coffee Cake with Chocolate Pecan Streusel

I created this decadent coffee cake for an article I wrote for Bon Appetit Magazine. It's an old-fashioned coffee cake, updated with orange, pecans and chocolate chips. It is perfect for picnics, brunches and potlucks.

Variation

Substitute walnuts for the pecans.

Preheat oven to 350°F (180°C)
13-by 9-inch (3 L) metal baking pan,
lined with parchment or waxed paper, greased

Streusel

1½ cups	packed light brown sugar	375 mL
1 tbsp	ground cinnamon	15 mL
⅓ cup	unsalted butter, chilled and cut into pieces	75 mL
1½ cups	coarsely chopped pecans	375 mL
1 cup	semisweet chocolate chips	250 mL

Cake

3 cups	all-purpose flour	750 mL
1½ tsp	baking soda	7 mL
1½ tsp	baking powder	7 mL
¾ cup	butter, at room temperature	175 mL
1⅓ cups	granulated sugar	325 mL
3	eggs	3
1½ tsp	grated orange zest	7 mL
1½ tsp	vanilla	7 mL
1½ cups	sour cream	375 mL
¼ cup	freshly squeezed orange juice	50 mL
	Confectioner's (icing) sugar (optional)	

1. *Streusel:* In a medium bowl, whisk together brown sugar and cinnamon. Add butter and rub in with fingertips until mixture holds together in small, moist clumps. Mix in pecans and chocolate chips. Set aside.

2. *Cake:* In a medium bowl, stir together flour, baking soda and baking powder.

3. In a large bowl, using electric mixer, beat butter and sugar until light and fluffy. Beat in eggs, one at a time, beating well after each addition. Beat in orange zest and vanilla. Stir in flour mixture alternately with sour cream, making three additions of flour mixture and two of sour cream. Stir in orange juice.

4. Spread half of the batter in prepared pan. Sprinkle with half of the streusel. Drop remaining batter over top by heaping tablespoons (15 mL), carefully spreading to make an even layer. Sprinkle with remaining streusel.

5. Bake in preheated oven for 30 minutes. Lay a sheet of foil loosely over pan to keep topping from browning too quickly. Bake for 35 minutes longer or until a tester inserted into center of cake comes out clean. Remove foil.

6. Let cake cool in pan on rack for 20 minutes. Serve warm or at room temperature. Lightly dust cake with confectioner's sugar, if desired.

Walnut Chocolate Chip Cake

Although this cake is rich, it's slightly sweet with a subtle maple flavor from the walnuts and brown sugar. I love it with a cup of tea.

Variation
Substitute pecans for the walnuts.

Preheat oven to 350°F (180°C)
10-inch (4 L) tube pan, greased and floured

4 cups	all-purpose flour	1 L
2 tsp	baking soda	10 mL
$\frac{1}{2}$ tsp	salt	2 mL
1 cup	unsalted butter, at room temperature	250 mL
1 cup	packed light brown sugar	250 mL
1 cup	granulated sugar	250 mL
4	eggs	4
2 cups	sour cream	500 mL
2 tsp	vanilla	10 mL
1 cup	walnut pieces	250 mL
1 cup	semisweet chocolate chips	250 mL
	Confectioner's (icing) sugar (optional)	

1. In a large bowl, combine flour, baking soda and salt.

2. In a large bowl, using electric mixer, beat butter and brown and granulated sugars until light and fluffy. Beat in eggs, one at a time, beating well after each addition. Beat in sour cream and vanilla. Add flour mixture, beating just until smooth. Stir in nuts and chocolate chips.

3. Spread batter in prepared pan. Bake in preheated oven for 70 minutes or until golden and a tester inserted into center comes out clean. Remove from pan and let cool completely on rack. Dust cooled cake with confectioner's sugar, if desired.

Cookies

Almond Caramel Bars

If you love buttery flavor, nutty crunch, chewy caramel and chocolate chip sensations all in one bite, then you will love these bars! Take heed: they are dangerously habit forming.

Tips

Wait until the crust has been baking in the oven for 10 to 15 minutes before preparing the caramel. Otherwise the caramel will thicken too quickly to spread on the baked crust.

For true caramel lovers, you can double the filling for an extra-gooey bar.

Variation

Substitute coarsely chopped macadamia nuts or walnuts for the almonds.

Preheat oven to 350°F (180°C)
13-by 9-inch (3 L) metal baking pan, greased
Candy thermometer

2 cups	all-purpose flour	500 mL
¾ cup	unsalted butter, at room temperature	175 mL
½ cup	packed light brown sugar	125 mL
½ tsp	vanilla	2 mL
¼ tsp	salt	1 mL
2 cups	coarsely chopped almonds	500 mL
Filling		
6 tbsp	unsalted butter	90 mL
¾ cup	packed light brown sugar	175 mL
¾ cup	light corn syrup	175 mL
Pinch	salt	Pinch
Topping		
2 cups	semisweet chocolate chips	500 mL

1. In a food processor fitted with a metal blade, combine flour, butter, brown sugar, vanilla and salt. Process until mixture comes together and just starts to form a ball. Press evenly into prepared pan. Sprinkle almonds over dough. Bake in preheated oven for 20 to 25 minutes or until golden brown.

2. *Filling:* In a heavy saucepan over medium heat, melt butter. Stir in brown sugar, corn syrup and salt. Simmer, stirring often, for about 5 minutes or until it reaches the soft-ball stage, 240°F (116°C) on a candy thermometer. Pour over baked crust, spreading evenly.

3. *Topping:* Sprinkle chocolate chips over caramel. Let cool and refrigerate until caramel is firm. (This also makes cutting easier.) Remove from pan and cut into bars.

Banana Blondies with Chocolate Chips and Walnuts

My kids like to call these Monkey Bars. The bananas bring out the best in their behavior. These bars are a superb combination of banana bread and chocolate chip cookie. They are an ideal alternative to traditional brownies.

Tip

For a more intense walnut flavor, toast the nuts before adding to the batter. Simply spread the nuts on a rimmed baking sheet and bake in a preheated 350°F (180°C) oven until lightly browned and fragrant, about 8 to 10 minutes. Let cool before mixing into batter.

Variations

You can substitute pecans for the walnuts. Of, if you're not a nut fan, omit them altogether.

Preheat oven to 350°F (180°C)
13-by 9-inch (3 L) metal baking pan, lined with foil and greased

2 cups	all-purpose flour	500 mL
2 tsp	baking powder	10 mL
1/4 tsp	salt	1 mL
3/4 cup	unsalted butter, at room temperature	175 mL
2/3 cup	granulated sugar	150 mL
2/3 cup	packed light brown sugar	150 mL
1 tsp	vanilla	5 mL
1	egg	1
1 cup	mashed ripe bananas (about 2 large)	250 mL
2 cups	semisweet chocolate chips	500 mL
1 cup	walnut pieces (see Tip, left)	250 mL

1. In a medium bowl, combine flour, baking powder and salt.

2. In a large bowl, using electric mixer, beat butter and granulated and brown sugars until light and fluffy. Beat in vanilla. Add egg and bananas, beating well. Add flour mixture and beat just until combined. Fold in chocolate chips and walnuts.

3. Spread batter in prepared pan. Bake in preheated oven for 30 to 35 minutes or until light golden brown and starting to pull away from sides of pan. The center will still be slightly soft to the touch.

4. Let cool completely in pan on rack. Cut into bars.

Brown Sugar Shortbread

These crunchy little cookies make a great accompaniment to a cup of tea or a bowl of ice cream. When I am in the mood for something crunchy and lightly sweet, these fit the bill.

Variations

You can omit the walnuts or substitute pecans, if you prefer.

Preheat oven to 350°F (180°C)
Baking sheets, lined with parchment paper

2 cups	all-purpose flour	500 mL
1/4 tsp	salt	1 mL
1 cup	unsalted butter, at room temperature	250 mL
1 cup	packed light brown sugar	250 mL
1	egg yolk	1
2 tsp	vanilla	10 mL
3/4 cup	semisweet chocolate chips	175 mL
1/2 cup	coarsely chopped walnuts	125 mL
	Granulated sugar, for rolling	

1. In a medium bowl, combine flour and salt.

2. In a large bowl, using electric mixer, beat butter and brown sugar until fluffy. Beat in egg yolk and vanilla. Add flour mixture and beat until smooth. Stir in chocolate chips and walnuts.

3. Using a small cookie scoop or tablespoon (15 mL), scoop dough into balls. Roll in granulated sugar. Place sugared cookies on prepared baking sheets, about 2 inches (5 cm) apart. Using the heel of your hand, press down lightly on top of each cookie, flattening into a disk. Don't worry if they aren't perfectly flat; this adds to their rustic appearance. Bake in preheated oven for 15 to 17 minutes or until light golden brown and firm to the touch. Let cool on pans on rack.

Butterscotch Pecan Chocolate Chip Blondies

Let's raise the bar a few notches. This scrumptious cookie bar is easy to prepare and the results are above one's personal best. Try it and see for yourself.

Tips

Butterscotch extract can be found at specialty food stores and some well-stocked grocery and health food stores.

To toast pecans: Preheat oven to 350°F (180°C). Spread pecans on baking sheet, lined with parchment paper, and bake for 8 to 10 minutes or until lightly browned.

Variations

Substitute walnuts for pecans or omit nuts altogether, if desired.

Preheat oven to 350°F (180°C)
13-by 9-inch (3 L) metal baking pan, greased

2½ cups	all-purpose flour	625 mL
1 tbsp	baking powder	15 mL
¼ tsp	salt	1 mL
1 cup	unsalted butter, melted	250 mL
3 cups	packed light brown sugar	750 mL
2 tsp	butterscotch extract (see Tips, left)	10 mL
1 tsp	vanilla	5 mL
4	eggs	4
2 cups	semisweet chocolate chips	500 mL
1 cup	coarsely chopped pecans, toasted (see Tips, left)	250 mL

1. In a medium bowl, combine flour, baking powder and salt.

2. In a large bowl, using electric mixer, beat melted butter and brown sugar until smooth. Add butterscotch extract and vanilla, beating well. Add eggs, one at a time, beating well after each addition. Add flour mixture and beat just until combined. Fold in chocolate chips and pecans.

3. Spread batter in prepared pan. Bake in preheated oven for 40 to 45 minutes or until browned and starting to pull away from sides of pan. Center will still be slightly soft to the touch. Let cool in pan on rack. Cut into bars.

Chocolate Cappuccino Chip Cookies

Need to add some octane to your day? Here's your coffee disguised in another form. These cookies are rich, sweet and a tasty treat — perfect when you need an afternoon pick-me-up.

Variation

Substitute milk chocolate chips for the semisweet chocolate chips.

Preheat oven to 350°F (180°C)
Baking sheets, lined with parchment paper

2½ cups	all-purpose flour	625 mL
½ cup	unsweetened Dutch-process cocoa powder, sifted	125 mL
1½ tbsp	ground cinnamon	22 mL
1 tbsp	instant coffee granules	15 mL
2 tsp	finely ground coffee	10 mL
1 tsp	baking powder	5 mL
1 tsp	baking soda	5 mL
¼ tsp	salt	1 mL
1 cup	unsalted butter, at room temperature	250 mL
1½ cups	granulated sugar	375 mL
1 cup	packed brown sugar	250 mL
1 tsp	vanilla	5 mL
2	eggs	2
2 cups	semisweet chocolate chips	500 mL

1. In a medium bowl, combine flour, cocoa powder, cinnamon, instant coffee granules, finely ground coffee, baking powder, baking soda and salt.

2. In a large bowl, using electric mixer, beat butter and granulated and brown sugars until light and fluffy. Beat in vanilla. Add eggs, one at a time, beating well after each addition. Add flour mixture and beat just until combined. Fold in chocolate chips.

3. Scooping dough with a ¼-cup (50 mL) ice cream scoop or by heaping tablespoons (15 mL), place dough on prepared baking sheets, about 3 inches (7.5 cm) apart. Bake in preheated oven for 12 minutes or until cookies are puffed and just slightly firm to the touch. They will still look somewhat undercooked. Let cool completely on pans on racks.

Oat Bars

When you are in the mood for something sweet, buttery and full of chocolate but don't want to expend much effort, these are the cookies for you. They are a one-bowl wonder.

Tip
To make these bars even easier, melt the butter in a microwave-safe mixing bowl or glass dish. Then add the remaining ingredients to the same dish.

Preheat oven to 350°F (180°C)
13-by 9-inch (3 L) metal baking pan,
lined with parchment paper, greased

1 cup	packed dark brown sugar	250 mL
3/4 cup	unsalted butter, melted	175 mL
3 tbsp	light corn syrup	45 mL
1/2 tsp	vanilla	2 mL
1/4 tsp	salt	1 mL
3 cups	old-fashioned rolled oats	750 mL
1 cup	semisweet chocolate chips	250 mL

1. In a large bowl, combine brown sugar, melted butter, corn syrup, vanilla and salt. Add oats and chocolate chips, mixing well.

2. Press dough into prepared pan. Bake in preheated oven for 20 to 25 minutes or until browned but not too dark. It will still be soft to the touch but will harden when it cools. Let cool in pan on rack. Cut into bars.

Chocolate Chip Spice Bars with Maple Glaze

Makes 16 bars

These bars are tasty to the nth degree. Don't let the ingredient list deter you. The flavors will continue to enhance the bars hours after baking. The combination of spices, chocolate and a maple glaze makes this cookie quite the taste sensation. Light and dark brown sugars add a deeper, more complex flavor.

Preheat oven to 350°F (180°C)
13-by 9-inch (3 L) metal baking pan,
lined with parchment paper, greased

1¾ cups	all-purpose flour	425 mL
2 tsp	ground cinnamon	10 mL
2 tsp	ground ginger	10 mL
1 tsp	ground allspice	5 mL
¾ tsp	baking soda	4 mL
¾ tsp	baking powder	4 mL
½ tsp	ground nutmeg	2 mL
¼ tsp	salt	1 mL
½ cup	unsalted butter, at room temperature	125 mL
¾ cup	packed light brown sugar	175 mL
½ cup	packed dark brown sugar	125 mL
¼ cup	strong brewed coffee, at room temperature	50 mL
2	eggs	2
1 cup	raisins	250 mL
¾ cup	semisweet chocolate chips	175 mL

Glaze

1½ cups	confectioner's (icing) sugar, sifted	375 mL
⅓ cup	milk	75 mL
½ tsp	maple extract	2 mL

1. In a medium bowl, combine flour, cinnamon, ginger, allspice, baking soda, baking powder, nutmeg and salt.

2. In a large bowl, using electric mixer, beat butter and light and dark brown sugars until light and fluffy. Stir in coffee. Add eggs, one at a time, beating well after each addition. Add flour mixture, beating on low speed until combined. Stir in raisins and chocolate chips.

3. Spread batter in prepared pan. Bake in preheated oven for 25 minutes or until top is just firm to the touch. Let cool in pan on rack.

4. *Glaze:* In a medium bowl, combine confectioner's sugar, milk and maple extract, whisking until smooth. When bars are almost cool, spread glaze over top. Let cool until glaze is set. Cut into bars.

Chocolate Cherry Biscotti

*Over the years, I have
developed many recipes for
biscotti (there are no bad
biscotti), but this is one of
my favorites. This version
was created for an article I
wrote on biscotti in* Cooking
Light Magazine.

Variations

If you don't have dried
cherries, dried cranberries
work really well.

You can also add $\frac{1}{2}$ cup
(125 mL) chopped toasted
almonds, if desired.

Preheat oven to 350°F (180°C)
Baking sheets, lined with parchment paper

3 cups	all-purpose flour	750 mL
$\frac{1}{4}$ tsp	salt	1 mL
1 cup	granulated sugar	250 mL
3	eggs	3
2 tbsp	vegetable oil	25 mL
2 tsp	vanilla	10 mL
$1\frac{1}{2}$ tsp	almond extract	7 mL
1 cup	semisweet chocolate chips	250 mL
$\frac{2}{3}$ cup	dried sour cherries	150 mL

1. In a medium bowl, combine flour and salt.

2. In a large bowl, using electric mixer, beat sugar and
   eggs until thickened and pale, about 4 minutes. Add
   oil, vanilla and almond extract, beating just until
   blended. Add flour mixture, beating on low speed
   just until blended. Stir in chocolate chips and cherries.

3. Divide dough in half. Turn out dough onto prepared
   baking sheets. Shape each half into a 10-inch (25 cm)
   long log and flatten to 1-inch (2.5 cm) thickness.
   Bake in preheated oven for 25 to 30 minutes or until
   lightly browned. Transfer logs to rack. Let cool for 10
   minutes. Reduce oven temperature to 325°F (160°C).

4. Transfer logs to a cutting board. Cut each log
   diagonally into $\frac{1}{2}$-inch (1 cm) slices. Place slices,
   cut side down, on baking sheet. Bake for 15 to
   20 minutes longer or until golden and toasted.
   The biscotti will be slightly soft in center but will
   harden as they cool. Transfer to racks and let
   cool completely.

Chocolate Chip Butterscotch Cookies

Although this recipe makes a lot of cookies, they freeze beautifully so that you always have cookies at the ready. But they're so melt-in-your-mouth good, they'll probably never make it to the freezer. We named these cookies Jay's Addiction at our bakery because my husband, Jay, can never get enough of them!

Tip

Make sure you don't overbake the cookies as they really do need to be slightly underbaked for best results.

Variation

Omit the butterscotch baking chips, increasing semisweet chocolate chips to 2$\frac{1}{3}$ cups (575 mL).

Preheat oven to 350°F (180°C)
Baking sheets, lined with parchment paper

3$\frac{1}{3}$ cups	all-purpose flour	825 mL
2 tsp	ground cinnamon	10 mL
1 tsp	ground ginger	5 mL
1 tsp	baking soda	5 mL
$\frac{1}{2}$ tsp	ground nutmeg	2 mL
$\frac{3}{4}$ cup	unsalted butter, at room temperature	175 mL
1 cup	packed light brown sugar	250 mL
$\frac{2}{3}$ cup	granulated sugar	150 mL
2	eggs	2
2 tsp	vanilla	10 mL
1$\frac{1}{2}$ cups	semisweet chocolate chips	375 mL
$\frac{2}{3}$ cup	butterscotch chips	150 mL
2 cups	confectioner's (icing) sugar	500 mL

1. In a small bowl, combine flour, cinnamon, ginger, baking soda and nutmeg.

2. In a medium bowl, using electric mixer, beat butter and brown and granulated sugars until light and fluffy. Add eggs, one at a time, beating well after each addition. Beat in vanilla. Add flour mixture, beating just until combined. Fold in chocolate and butterscotch chips.

3. Scoop dough by tablespoons (15 mL) and roll in confectioner's sugar. Place cookies on prepared baking sheets, about 2 inches (5 cm) apart. Bake in preheated oven for 12 to 14 minutes or until puffed and pale golden. They will still be soft to the touch in center and look somewhat undercooked. Let cool completely on pans on racks.

Chocolate Almond Drops

**Makes 60
small cookies**

*These cookies are fabulous
served with vanilla bean ice
cream or a cup of espresso.
The recipe goes together
in a snap and yields a richly
flavored cookie. As you can
see, this makes a large batch
of cookies. They freeze so
well that I always keep
some on hand. Louie, this
one's for you.*

Tip

If you prefer a smaller quantity
of cookies, you can easily cut
the recipe in half.

Preheat oven to 350°F (180°C)
Baking sheets, lined with parchment paper

3 cups	whole almonds, toasted (see Tips, page 33)	750 mL
1¼ cups	granulated sugar	300 mL
1 cup	semisweet chocolate chips	250 mL
4	egg whites	4
2 tsp	almond extract	10 mL

1. In a food processor fitted with a metal blade, grind almonds and sugar. Add chocolate chips and pulse until finely ground. Add egg whites and almond extract. Blend until smooth.

2. Drop by tablespoons (15 mL) or 1¼-inch (3 cm) cookie scoop onto prepared baking sheets, about 2 inches (5 cm) apart. Bake in preheated oven for 35 minutes or until firm, puffed and slightly cracked. Let cookies cool completely on pans on racks. Store in an airtight container.

Chocolate Brittle Bars

*These bars are more confection
than cookie. "To die for" is
an understatement when
describing the flavor and
sensation of these treats.
Making them is a lot of fun,
too. I always let my artistic
expression emerge when
drizzling chocolate.*

Tip
Look for 10-oz (300 g) bags
of English toffee bits in
the baking section of the
grocery store.

Variation
Substitute shelled pistachios
for the almonds.

Preheat oven to 350°F (180°C)
*17-by 11-inch (45 by 28 cm) rimmed baking sheet,
lined with parchment paper*

2 cups	all-purpose flour	500 mL
1/4 tsp	salt	1 mL
1 cup plus 1 tbsp	unsalted butter, at room temperature	265 mL
1 cup	lightly packed light brown sugar	250 mL
1 tsp	vanilla	5 mL
1 1/2 cups	English toffee bits (see Tip, left)	375 mL
2 1/2 cups	semisweet chocolate chips	625 mL
1 1/2 cups	almonds, toasted and chopped (see Tips, page 33)	375 mL

1. In a medium bowl, combine flour and salt.

2. In a large bowl, beat butter and sugar. Beat in vanilla.
   Stir in flour mixture just until dough is smooth.
   Stir in English toffee bits.

3. Press dough onto prepared baking sheet. Bake in
   preheated oven for 25 to 30 minutes or until dark
   golden brown. Let cool on pan on rack for 5 minutes.
   Sprinkle top with chocolate chips. When chocolate
   chips look soft and shiny, spread them over surface
   with a spatula. Sprinkle with chopped almonds.
   Refrigerate until chocolate is firm, then break
   into pieces.

Chocolate Chip Cherry Bars

Fred and Ginger, Dean and Jerry, John and Yoko, and chocolate and cherries. Can you mention one of these without including the other? I think not. This recipe pairs these inseparable partners for yet another encore with award-winning results. They make a great after-school snack.

Variation

Substitute raisins or dried cranberries for the cherries.

Preheat oven to 350°F (180°C)

13-by 9-inch (3 L) metal baking pan, greased

2¼ cups	all-purpose flour	550 mL
¾ tsp	baking soda	4 mL
¾ tsp	baking powder	4 mL
½ tsp	ground cinnamon	2 mL
¼ tsp	salt	1 mL
¾ cup	unsalted butter, at room temperature	175 mL
2¼ cups	packed light brown sugar	550 mL
3	eggs	3
1 tbsp	vanilla	15 mL
4½ cups	old-fashioned rolled oats	1.125 L
2 cups	semisweet chocolate chips	500 mL
1 cup	dried sour cherries	250 mL

1. In a medium bowl, combine flour, baking soda, baking powder, cinnamon and salt.

2. In a large bowl, using electric mixer, beat butter and sugar until light and fluffy. Add eggs, one at a time, beating well after each addition. Beat in vanilla. Stir in flour mixture. Add oats, mixing until moistened. Stir in chocolate chips and cherries.

3. Spread batter in prepared pan. Bake in preheated oven for 25 to 30 minutes or until golden and starting to pull away from sides of pan. Center will still be slightly soft to the touch. Let cool completely in pan on rack. Cut into bars.

Chocolate Mint Sandwich Cookies

These rustic-looking cookie sandwiches are absolutely delightful. Not too sweet, yet full of bittersweet chocolate mint flavor, they are well worth the effort.

Tip
These cookies are best eaten the day they are made but will keep frozen for up to 3 weeks.

Preheat oven to 350°F (180°C)
Baking sheets, lined with parchment paper

1½ cups	all-purpose flour	375 mL
¾ cup	unsweetened Dutch-process cocoa powder, sifted	175 mL
¼ tsp	salt	1 mL
¾ cup	unsalted butter, at room temperature	175 mL
1 cup	granulated sugar	250 mL
1	egg	1
1 tsp	vanilla	5 mL
	Granulated sugar for topping	

Filling

¼ cup	whipping (35%) cream	50 mL
1 cup	semisweet chocolate chips	250 mL
½ tsp	peppermint extract	2 mL

1. In a medium bowl, combine flour, cocoa powder and salt.

2. In a large bowl, using electric mixer, beat butter and sugar until light and fluffy. Add egg and vanilla, beating until smooth. Add flour mixture and beat just until blended.

3. Drop by tablespoons (15 mL) or 1¼-inch (3 cm) cookie scoop on prepared baking sheets, about 2 inches (5 cm) apart. Dip the heel of your hand in sugar and lightly flatten cookies into 2-inch (5 cm) rounds. Bake in preheated oven for 12 to 15 minutes or until dry to the touch. Let cool completely on pans on racks.

4. *Filling:* In a microwave-safe bowl, combine cream and chocolate chips. Microwave on High for 1 to 1½ minutes, stirring every 30 seconds, until chocolate is shiny and almost melted. Stir until smooth. Stir in peppermint extract. Set aside to cool slightly.

5. Spread filling on half of the cookies. Top with remaining cookies. Refrigerate until filling is firm, about 20 minutes.

Chocolate Chip Orange Biscotti

These biscotti are a very popular item in our gift baskets. Orange and chocolate leave an everlasting impression on the taste buds. My buds are partial to this combo. Properly stored in an airtight container, they will last for two months.

Preheat oven to 350°F (180°C)
Baking sheets, lined with parchment paper

2¾ cups	all-purpose flour	675 mL
1 cup	granulated sugar	250 mL
2 tsp	baking powder	10 mL
1 tbsp	vegetable oil	15 mL
1 tbsp	orange extract	15 mL
2 tsp	grated orange zest	10 mL
1 tsp	vanilla	5 mL
3	eggs	3
1 cup	semisweet chocolate chips	250 mL

1. In a medium bowl, combine flour, sugar and baking powder.

2. In a large bowl, using electric mixer, beat oil, orange extract, orange zest, vanilla and eggs until blended. Add flour mixture, beating until well blended. Stir in chocolate chips.

3. Divide dough in half. Turn out dough onto prepared baking sheets. Shape each half into 10-inch (25 cm) long logs and flatten to 1-inch (2.5 cm) thickness. Bake in preheated oven for 25 to 30 minutes or until lightly browned. Transfer logs to a rack. Let cool for 10 minutes. Reduce oven temperature to 325°F (160°C).

4. Transfer logs to cutting board. Cut each log diagonally into ½-inch (1 cm) slices. Place slices, cut side down, on baking sheet. Bake for 15 to 20 minutes longer or until golden and toasted. The biscotti will be soft in center but will harden as they cool. Transfer to racks and let cool completely.

Chocolate-Dipped Coconut Macaroons

Imagine the Alps sitting on a river of chocolate and you will get an idea of what this cookie looks like — a huge mound of coconut perched atop a foundation of chocolate. It's like your favorite candy bar, but better!

Tip

Store macaroons in an airtight container at cool room temperature so the chocolate won't melt.

Preheat oven to 350°F (180°C)
Baking sheets, lined with parchment paper

3 cups	packed shredded sweetened coconut (about 15 oz/435 g)	750 mL
1/2 cup	granulated sugar	125 mL
6 tbsp	all-purpose flour	90 mL
4	egg whites	4
2 tsp	vanilla	10 mL
1/2 cup	semisweet chocolate chips	125 mL
10 oz	semisweet or bittersweet chocolate, chopped	300 g

1. In a large bowl, using electric mixer, combine coconut, sugar and flour. Add egg whites and vanilla, beating until well mixed. Stir in chocolate chips.

2. Using a 2-inch (5 cm) diameter ice cream scoop or 1/4-cup (50 mL) measure, place mounds of dough on prepared baking sheets, about 2 inches (5 cm) apart. Bake in preheated oven for 15 to 18 minutes or until tops are puffed and golden brown. Cookies will still be moist in center. Let cool completely on pans on racks.

3. In a microwave-safe bowl, microwave chopped chocolate on Medium for 3 to 4 minutes, stirring often, until melted, smooth and warm. Do not overheat. Dip bottoms of cooled macaroons into melted chocolate. Place on baking sheets lined with parchment paper or waxed paper. Refrigerate until chocolate is set.

Chocolate Chip Meringues

These crisp little gems are low in both fat and calories. They are delicious, with melt-in-your-mouth goodness, and completely addictive for all the right reasons.

Tip

For a decorative look that's also delicious, lightly dust meringues with unsweetened cocoa powder or ground cinnamon before baking. Also, I like these cookies when they are crisp on the outside and just slightly soft and chewy in the center. To achieve crispy yet soft meringues, slightly underbake the cookies by a few minutes.

Preheat oven to 300°F (150°C)
Baking sheets, lined with parchment paper

4	egg whites	4
1/4 tsp	cream of tartar	1 mL
1 cup	granulated sugar	250 mL
3/4 cup	miniature semisweet chocolate chips	175 mL

1. In a large bowl, using electric mixer, beat egg whites and cream of tartar at high speed until soft peaks form. Add sugar, 1 tbsp (15 mL) at a time, beating until peaks are stiff and glossy. Fold in chocolate chips.

2. Drop by rounded tablespoons (15 mL) on prepared baking sheets, about 2 inches (5 cm) apart. Bake in preheated oven for 40 to 45 minutes or until crisp. Let cookies cool completely on pans on racks. Store in an airtight container for several days.

Six-Layer Bars *(page 105)*

Overleaf: Butterscotch Pecan Chocolate Chip Blondies *(page 83)*, The Quintessential Chocolate Chip Cookie *(page 108)* and Chocolate-Dipped Coconut Macaroons *(page 95)*

Cowgirl Cookies

*Cowgirls of the world, unite!
This recipe is for you. Soft
and chewy, these cookies are
full of oats, raisins, chocolate
chips and crisp rice cereal.
Buckaroos will enjoy them, too.*

Variation

Substitute dried cranberries
for the raisins.

Preheat oven to 350°F (180°C)
Baking sheets, lined with parchment paper

1½ cups	all-purpose flour	375 mL
1 tsp	baking powder	5 mL
¼ tsp	salt	1 mL
1 cup	unsalted butter, melted and cooled slightly	250 mL
1 cup	packed light brown sugar	250 mL
½ cup	granulated sugar	125 mL
2	eggs	2
1 tsp	vanilla	5 mL
2½ cups	old-fashioned rolled oats	625 mL
2 cups	semisweet chocolate chips	500 mL
1½ cups	crisp rice cereal	375 mL
1 cup	raisins	250 mL

1. In a medium bowl, combine flour, baking powder and salt.

2. In a large bowl, using electric mixer, beat melted butter and brown and granulated sugars until blended. Add eggs, one at a time, beating well after each addition. Beat in vanilla. Add flour mixture and beat just until combined. Stir in oats, chocolate chips, cereal and raisins.

3. Drop by ¼-cup (50 mL) measure on prepared baking sheets, about 2 inches (5 cm) apart. Bake in preheated oven for 14 to 16 minutes or until puffed, light golden and somewhat soft to the touch. Let cool completely on pans on racks.

Maple Pecan Muffins with
Chocolate Chips *(page 132)*
and Chocolate Chip Cranberry
Muffins *(page 129)*

Double Chocolate Mint Chunkers

I have watched people clamor over each other for these cookies. A dark chocolate butter cookie studded with semisweet and mint chocolate chips makes for a treat that's worth fighting for.

Tips

These cookies are best the day they are made. They don't freeze particularly well.

You can find mint baking chips in most well-stocked grocery stores. If you can't find them, substitute chocolate mint chips.

Variation

Substitute semisweet chocolate chips for the mint baking chips.

Preheat oven to 350°F (180°C)
Baking sheets, lined with parchment paper

2 cups	all-purpose flour	500 mL
1¼ cups	unsweetened Dutch-process cocoa powder, sifted	300 mL
1 tsp	baking powder	5 mL
¼ tsp	salt	1 mL
1¼ cups	unsalted butter, at room temperature	300 mL
2 cups	granulated sugar	500 mL
2	eggs	2
2 tsp	vanilla	10 mL
1 tsp	peppermint extract	5 mL
1½ cups	semisweet chocolate chips	375 mL
1½ cups	mint baking chips (see Tips, left)	375 mL

1. In a medium bowl, combine flour, cocoa powder, baking powder and salt.

2. In a large bowl, using electric mixer, beat butter and sugar until light and fluffy. Add eggs, one at a time, beating well after each addition. Add vanilla and peppermint extract, mixing well. Add flour mixture and beat just until blended. Stir in chocolate and mint chips.

3. Using 2 tbsp (25 mL) or ⅛-cup (25 mL) measure or ice cream scoop, drop dough on prepared baking sheets, about 3 inches (7.5 cm) apart. Bake in preheated oven for 16 to 17 minutes or until cookies are puffed and starting to crack. They will still be soft to the touch in the center and look somewhat undercooked. Let cool completely on pans on racks.

Double Fudge Espresso Brownies

This is a great recipe when you want an awesome brownie but don't want to have to go to a lot of work. They're very fast to make, so you can satisfy that chocolate craving in no time.

Tip

For a decorative garnish, lightly dust cooled cut brownies with confectioner's (icing) sugar.

Variation

Add ⅔ cup (150 mL) dried sour cherries to batter.

Preheat oven to 350°F (180°C)
13-by 9-inch (3 L) metal baking pan, lined with parchment paper, greased

1 cup	all-purpose flour	250 mL
¾ cup	unsweetened Dutch-process cocoa powder, sifted	175 mL
2 tsp	finely ground coffee	10 mL
1½ tsp	baking powder	7 mL
1 tsp	instant coffee granules	5 mL
¼ tsp	salt	1 mL
1 cup	unsalted butter, melted	250 mL
1 cup	granulated sugar	250 mL
1 cup	packed light brown sugar	250 mL
3	eggs	3
1½ tsp	vanilla	7 mL
½ tsp	almond extract	2 mL
1 cup	semisweet chocolate chips	250 mL

1. In a medium bowl, combine flour, cocoa powder, ground coffee, baking powder, instant coffee granules and salt.

2. In a large bowl, using electric mixer, beat melted butter and granulated and brown sugars until blended. Add eggs, one at a time, beating well after each addition. Beat in vanilla and almond extract. Add flour mixture and beat until blended.

3. Spread batter in prepared pan. Sprinkle with chocolate chips, lightly pressing into surface. Bake in preheated oven for 30 minutes or until still somewhat soft to the touch and a tester inserted into center has moist crumbs clinging to it. Let cool completely in pan on rack. Cut into squares.

Chocolate Chip Madeleines

*Vive la France for sharing these
infamous little cake-like cookies,
made popular by Marcel
Proust in his* Remembrance
of Things Past. *You won't
have to travel to France to
find these gems, because
these Madeleines are imported
right from your kitchen. Look
for Madeleine pans in kitchen
stores and catalogs.*

Tip

This dough will keep very well
in the refrigerator for up to
1 week, so bake only what
you need and refrigerate the
rest. Cookies are best eaten
the day they are made. Store
in an airtight container.

Preheat oven to 350°F (180°C)
Madeleine pans, greased

1 cup	unsalted butter, at room temperature	250 mL
2¼ cups	confectioner's (icing) sugar, sifted	550 mL
4	eggs	4
1 tbsp	grated orange zest	15 mL
½ tsp	vanilla	2 mL
½ tsp	almond extract	2 mL
1⅔ cups	all-purpose flour	400 mL
¾ cup	semisweet chocolate chips	175 mL
	Confectioner's (icing) sugar, for dusting	

1. In a bowl, using electric mixer, beat butter and sugar
   until light and fluffy (this might take a few minutes).
   Add eggs, one at a time, beating well after each
   addition. Add orange zest, vanilla and almond
   extract, beating until combined. Add flour, beating
   just until combined.

2. Scoop dough by scant tablespoons (15 mL) into
   prepared pans. Sprinkle each with about 1 tsp (5 mL)
   of the chocolate chips. Bake in preheated oven for
   10 minutes or until just barely firm to the touch.
   Cookies will be very pale in color.

3. Unmold cookies onto a sheet of parchment or waxed
   paper, either by carefully flipping over the pan or by
   gently using a wooden skewer (the chips might stick
   a bit when unmolding, but don't worry about this).
   Separate cookies and let cool completely. Dust with
   confectioner's sugar.

Pumpkin Chocolate Chip Cookies

These cookies are my son Noah's absolute favorite. We used to make them every Halloween but decided that they were too delicious to enjoy only once a year. There's only one trick for making these cookies year-round: maintain a supply of canned pumpkin in your pantry.

Variation

Add ³⁄₄ cup (175 mL) coarsely chopped walnuts.

Preheat oven to 350°F (180°C)
Baking sheets, lined with parchment paper

2 cups	all purpose-flour	500 mL
2 tsp	ground cinnamon	10 mL
1 tsp	baking soda	5 mL
¹⁄₈ tsp	salt	0.5 mL
1 cup	unsalted butter, at room temperature	250 mL
1 cup	granulated sugar	250 mL
½ cup	packed light brown sugar	125 mL
1	egg	1
1 cup	canned pumpkin purée (not pie filling)	250 mL
1 tsp	vanilla	5 mL
2 cups	semisweet chocolate chips	500 mL
	Granulated sugar, for rolling	

1. In a medium bowl, combine flour, cinnamon, baking soda and salt.

2. In a large bowl, using electric mixer, beat butter and granulated and brown sugars until fluffy. Beat in egg, mixing well. Add pumpkin and vanilla until blended. Add flour mixture and beat just until combined. Stir in chocolate chips.

3. Scoop dough by tablespoons (15 mL) and roll in sugar. Place balls on prepared baking sheets, about 2 inches (5 cm) apart. Bake in preheated oven for 10 to 12 minutes or until cookies are set around edges. Let cool completely on pans on racks.

...erry Chocolate Chip Bars

... that I
...eloped for an article in
Cooking Light Magazine.
*If you cut the bars into
16 portions, you have a
decadent but virtuous snack.
Personally, I prefer a larger
bar, despite the extra calories.*

Variation

Add ½ cup (125 mL) sliced
almonds with chocolate chips.

Preheat oven to 375°F (190°C)
*8-inch (2 L) square baking pan,
lined with parchment paper, greased*

1 cup	all-purpose flour	250 mL
1 cup	quick-cooking rolled oats	250 mL
½ tsp	baking soda	2 mL
½ tsp	salt	2 mL
⅓ cup	unsalted butter, at room temperature	75 mL
¾ cup	packed light brown sugar	175 mL
¾ cup	semisweet chocolate chips	175 mL
1	jar (10 oz/300 mL) seedless raspberry jam (1¼ cups/300 mL)	1

1. In a medium bowl, combine flour, oats, baking soda and salt.

2. In a large bowl, using electric mixer, beat butter and sugar until light and fluffy. Add flour mixture and beat until well blended (mixture will be crumbly).

3. Transfer ¾ cup (175 mL) of the dough to a bowl. Toss with chocolate chips and set aside. Press remaining dough into prepared pan. Spread evenly with jam. Sprinkle with chocolate chip mixture. Bake in preheated oven for 30 minutes or until golden brown. Let cool completely in pan on rack. Cut into squares.

Raspberry Chocolate Chip Cookies

These cookies are delicate, slightly sweet and make a perfect accompaniment to afternoon tea. At home, we call them Sydney Janes because the above adjectives describe my daughter, Sydney, to a tee.

Tip
These cookies freeze well for about 1 month in resealable freezer bags.

Variation
Substitute apricot jam for the raspberry.

Preheat oven to 350°F (180°C)
Baking sheets, lined with parchment paper

1 cup	unsalted butter, at room temperature	250 mL
2/3 cup	granulated sugar	150 mL
1 tsp	almond extract	5 mL
1/2 tsp	vanilla	2 mL
2 cups	all-purpose flour	500 mL
1/4 cup	raspberry jam	50 mL
	Semisweet chocolate chips	
	Confectioner's (icing) sugar	

1. In a large bowl, using electric mixer, beat butter and sugar until light and fluffy. Add almond extract and vanilla, beating until well mixed. Add flour and mix until incorporated.

2. Drop by tablespoonfuls (15 mL) or with $1\frac{1}{4}$-inch (3 cm) cookie scoop on prepared baking sheets, about 2 inches (2.5 cm) apart. (If using a spoon, roll scoops into balls in the palms of your hands.) Using your thumb or the end of a wooden spoon, make a well in the center of each cookie (pressing down three-quarters of the way through cookie). Using two small spoons, fill wells with jam and sprinkle three chocolate chips on top of each.

3. Bake in preheated oven for 15 minutes or until slightly firm to the touch but still somewhat pale in color. Let cool completely on pans on racks. Dust cooled cookies lightly with confectioner's sugar.

Rum Raisin Spoon Brownies

*These are small individual
brownie cookies, about the
size of a teaspoon. Though
bite-size, they're packed with
the punch of rum raisins
and chocolate.*

Preheat oven to 350°F (180°C)
Baking sheets, lined with parchment paper

8 oz	unsweetened chocolate, chopped	250 g
2 cups	semisweet chocolate chips, divided	500 mL
6 tbsp	unsalted butter	90 mL
¾ cup	raisins	175 mL
¼ cup	gold rum	50 mL
½ cup	all-purpose flour	125 mL
½ tsp	baking powder	2 mL
4	eggs	4
1½ cups	granulated sugar	375 mL
1 tsp	vanilla	5 mL

1. In a microwave-safe bowl, combine unsweetened chocolate, 1 cup (250 mL) of the chocolate chips and butter. Microwave on High for 2 minutes, stirring every 30 seconds, until chocolate is shiny and almost melted. Stir until smooth. Let cool slightly.

2. In a small microwave-safe bowl, combine raisins and rum. Microwave on High for 1 minute. Set aside to cool.

3. In a small bowl, mix together flour and baking powder.

4. In a large bowl, using electric mixer, beat eggs, sugar and vanilla until well combined. Add chocolate mixture, beating well. Add flour mixture and blend until smooth. Stir in raisin mixture. Stir in remaining chocolate chips. Refrigerate dough for 30 minutes to thicken.

5. Drop by tablespoons (15 mL) or with 1¼-inch (3 cm) cookie scoop on prepared pans, about 2 inches (5 cm) apart. Bake in preheated oven for 10 minutes or until puffed and cracked. Cookies will firm up when cool; do not overbake. Let cool completely on pans on racks.

Six-Layer Bars

My brother, Jon, and I grew up on these bars. Although there are many versions of this recipe, I like mine with chocolate, coconut and almonds. These are extremely easy to make — the perfect project for children or when you want dessert in a jiffy.

Tip
Store any leftover sweetened condensed milk in a covered container in the refrigerator. Try stirring it into coffee or tea for a real treat.

Variation
Substitute chopped macadamia nuts for the almonds.

Preheat oven to 350°F (180°C)
9-inch (2.5 L) square metal baking pan, greased

³/₄ cup	butter, melted	175 mL
1¹/₂ cups	graham cracker crumbs, cinnamon or regular	375 mL
1¹/₃ cups	sweetened condensed milk	325 mL
1¹/₂ cups	sweetened flaked coconut	375 mL
1¹/₂ cups	almonds, toasted and coarsely chopped (see Tips, page 33)	375 mL
1¹/₂ cups	semisweet chocolate chips	375 mL

1. Pour butter into prepared baking dish and sprinkle with graham cracker crumbs. Drizzle sweetened condensed milk over crumbs (spreading with a spatula, if necessary). Top with coconut, almonds and chocolate chips. With a spatula, press down lightly on top of bars to pack down ingredients.

2. Bake in preheated oven for 30 minutes or until lightly browned. Let cool completely in pan on rack. Cut into bars.

Slice-and-Bake Chocolate Chip Almond Cookies

These are fantastic to have on hand in the freezer. My husband, Jay, loves them for midnight snacks, but I love them for quick after-school treats or desserts.

Variation

Substitute chopped macadamia nuts for the almonds.

Baking sheets, lined with parchment paper

2¼ cups	all-purpose flour	550 mL
1 tsp	baking soda	5 mL
¼ tsp	salt	1 mL
1 cup	unsalted butter, at room temperature	250 mL
1 cup	granulated sugar	250 mL
½ cup	packed light brown sugar	125 mL
2	eggs	2
2 tsp	vanilla	10 mL
2 cups	semisweet chocolate chips	500 mL
1 cup	almonds, toasted and chopped (see Tips, page 33)	250 mL
½ cup	sweetened flaked coconut	125 mL

1. In a medium bowl, combine flour, baking soda and salt.

2. In a large bowl, using electric mixer, beat butter and granulated and brown sugars until light and fluffy. Add eggs, one at a time, beating well after each addition. Beat in vanilla. Add flour mixture. Beat just until combined. Stir in chocolate chips, almonds and coconut.

3. Scrape out dough onto a work surface lined with plastic wrap. With lightly floured hands, form into 3 logs. Roll up individually in plastic wrap, then wrap in layer of foil. Freeze until firm. Dough can be frozen for up to 2 months.

4. When ready to bake, preheat oven to 350°F (180°C). Unwrap dough and slice into ½-inch (1 cm) thick rounds. Place on prepared baking sheets. Bake for 11 minutes or until light golden brown around edges and still pale and soft to the touch in the center. Let cool on pans on rack.

Snickerdoodle Chip Biscotti

Makes 30 biscotti

This is a variation of a recipe that I created for Cooking Light Magazine. *It has a nice vanilla flavor to it, with a light cinnamon-sugar coating and, of course, chocolate chips. This is the ultimate cookie for dunking and munching.*

Preheat oven to 350°F (180°C)
Baking sheet, lined with parchment paper

2¾ cups	all-purpose flour	675 mL
2 tsp	baking powder	10 mL
¼ tsp	salt	1 mL
1 cup plus 2 tbsp	granulated sugar, divided	275 mL
1 tbsp	vegetable oil	15 mL
1 tsp	vanilla	5 mL
3	eggs	3
1 cup	semisweet chocolate chips	250 mL
1 tsp	ground cinnamon	5 mL
1	egg white	1

1. In a medium bowl, combine flour, baking powder and salt.

2. In a large bowl, using electric mixer, beat 1 cup (250 mL) of the sugar, oil, vanilla and eggs until blended. Add flour mixture. Beat until combined. Stir in chocolate chips.

3. Divide dough in half. Turn out dough onto prepared baking sheet. Shape each half into 10-inch (25 cm) long log and flatten to 1-inch (2.5 cm) thickness. Combine remaining sugar and cinnamon. Gently brush tops of logs with egg white and sprinkle with cinnamon-sugar topping.

4. Bake in preheated oven for 25 to 30 minutes or until lightly browned. Transfer logs to rack. Let cool for 10 minutes. Reduce oven temperature to 325°F (160°C).

5. Transfer logs to cutting board. Cut each diagonally into ½-inch (1 cm) slices. Place biscotti, cut side down, on baking sheet. Bake for 15 to 20 minutes longer or until golden and toasted. Biscotti will be slightly soft in center but will harden as they cool. Transfer to racks and let cool completely.

The Quintessential Chocolate Chip Cookie

Makes 29 cookies

I have made thousands of chocolate chip cookies in my life. They often take on a life of their own, coming out differently depending on ingredients used, time of year, altitude, oven temperature variations and, of course, my presence of mind. This recipe has never let me down — thus the boastful name. Your taste buds will appreciate the 100% pure ingredients and love that went into these melt-in-your-mouth cookies.

Variation

Substitute macadamia nuts for the walnuts.

Preheat oven to 350°F (180°C)
Baking sheets, lined with parchment paper

3 cups	all-purpose flour	750 mL
1 tsp	baking powder	5 mL
¼ tsp	salt	1 mL
1 cup	unsalted butter, at room temperature	250 mL
2⅓ cups	packed light brown sugar	575 mL
2 tsp	vanilla	10 mL
2	eggs	2
2⅓ cups	semisweet chocolate chips	575 mL
1½ cups	walnut pieces	375 mL

1. In a medium bowl, combine flour, baking powder and salt.

2. In a large bowl, using electric mixer, beat butter and sugar until light and fluffy. Add vanilla, mixing well. Add eggs, one at a time, beating well after each addition. Add flour mixture and beat just until combined. Fold in chocolate chips and walnuts.

3. Drop by ¼-cup (50 mL) measure on prepared baking sheets, about 2 inches (5 cm) apart. Bake in preheated oven for 15 to 20 minutes or until puffed and pale golden. Cookies will still be soft to the touch in center and look somewhat undercooked. Let cool completely on pans on racks.

Frozen Desserts

Banana Caramel Terrine

This is a fun way to serve vanilla ice cream with a fancy flair. Your guests will be eager to dig into the center filling of caramel, chocolate chips, walnuts and bananas.

Tip

Use a warm sharp knife (not wet) to slice the terrine.

Variations

Use Chocolate Caramel Sauce (see recipe, page 166) in place of the caramel sauce.

You can also substitute chocolate ice cream for the vanilla.

9-by 5-inch (2 L) metal loaf pan, lined with plastic wrap

4 cups	vanilla ice cream, slightly softened	1 L
1	banana, chopped into chunks	1
3/4 cup	walnuts, coarsely chopped	175 mL
1/2 cup	semisweet chocolate chips	125 mL
2/3 cup	caramel sauce, store-bought or homemade (see Chocolate Caramel Sauce, Variation, page 166)	150 mL

1. Spread half of the ice cream in bottom of prepared pan. Top with banana chunks. Sprinkle walnuts and chocolate chips over banana. With your hand or a spatula, lightly press top of terrine to pack down ingredients. Spread caramel sauce over walnuts. Carefully spread remaining ice cream over caramel.

2. Place a piece of plastic wrap directly on ice cream to cover. Gently press down on plastic wrap to smooth top. Freeze until frozen solid, preferably overnight.

3. Remove pan from freezer and carefully invert onto a cutting board or serving platter. Slice terrine and serve immediately.

Affogato

Tradition abounds in this Italian recipe, the name of which means "drowned ice." It can be thrown together in minutes. It is a perfect summertime dessert but equally appealing at other times of the year.

Tips

Look for almond syrup and other flavored syrups in the coffee aisle of your grocery store. Or check out local coffeehouses or shops; they usually carry a large selection.

This would be a great dessert to serve with Chocolate Chip Orange Biscotti (see recipe, page 94).

2 cups	vanilla ice cream	500 mL
1/3 cup	semisweet chocolate chips	75 mL
4 tsp	Kirsch liqueur	20 mL
4 tsp	almond syrup (see Tips, left)	20 mL
1 cup	hot strong brewed coffee	250 mL

1. Divide ice cream among four wine goblets. Sprinkle chocolate chips over ice cream. Drizzle Kirsch and almond syrup over top.

2. Pour $1/4$ cup (50 mL) of the hot coffee into each glass. Serve immediately.

Banana Chip Foster

I could sit and eat a bowl of this right now! Whoever thought bananas could taste this good? Use medium to large bananas, just barely ripe with a touch of green, and you'll see what I mean.

Tip

This recipe is fantastic served over buttermilk pancakes.

½ cup	unsalted butter	125 mL
¾ cup	packed light brown sugar	175 mL
¼ tsp	salt	1 mL
5	bananas, peeled and cut diagonally into 1-inch (2.5 cm) pieces	5
½ cup	dark rum	125 mL
2 cups	vanilla ice cream	500 mL
6 tbsp	semisweet chocolate chips	90 mL

1. In a large skillet over medium heat, melt butter. Stir in brown sugar and salt. Heat until foamy. Add bananas, stirring to coat. Cook for 1 minute. Add rum and cook for 5 minutes or until thickened and syrupy. Remove from heat and let cool for 10 minutes.

2. Scoop ice cream into six individual dishes. Spoon banana mixture over top. Sprinkle 1 tbsp (15 mL) of the chocolate chips over each serving. Serve immediately.

Chipwiches

These are better than store-bought ice cream sandwiches and very addictive. In fact, my children have been known to willingly do household chores for these chilly treats. They will keep, frozen in a resealable freezer bag, for a week or two.

Tips

I find that ice cream sandwiches work best with store-bought ice cream, unless you are going to serve them the day they are made.

You can make these ice cream sandwiches using a tube or roll of store-bought cookie dough. Simply slice or scoop dough into 16 portions and bake according to manufacturer's directions.

Variation

Substitute coffee or mint ice cream for the vanilla.

Baking sheet, lined with waxed paper

2 cups	vanilla ice cream, slightly softened	500 mL
16	freshly baked and cooled chocolate chip cookies (see The Quintessential Chocolate Chip Cookie, page 108)	16
1 cup	miniature semisweet chocolate chips	250 mL

1. Place a scoop of ice cream on a cookie. Top with another cookie, pressing down lightly so that ice cream spreads almost to edges. Repeat with remaining ice cream and cookies.

2. Place chocolate chips in a bowl. Stand 1 cookie sandwich on edge and roll across chocolate chips so that they adhere to surface of ice cream. Repeat with remaining cookie sandwiches.

3. Freeze sandwiches on prepared baking sheet for several hours or until ice cream is firm. Serve immediately or store in the freezer for 1 to 2 weeks.

Chocolate Rum Raisin Ice Cream

Makes 4 cups (1 L)

I have always been a huge fan of rum raisin ice cream. This is my version, with rum-infused raisins and morsels of chocolate chips submerged in dark chocolate ice cream.

Tip

Homemade ice cream will be somewhat softer in texture than store-bought. It is best served the day that it is made.

Ice cream maker

½ cup	raisins	125 mL
2 tbsp	gold rum	25 mL
1 cup	semisweet chocolate chips	250 mL
1½ cups	whipping (35%) cream, divided	375 mL
¾ cup	milk	175 mL
⅓ cup	superfine sugar	75 mL
1 cup	miniature semisweet chocolate chips	250 mL

1. In a small microwave-safe bowl, combine raisins and rum. Microwave on High for 60 seconds. Set aside to cool for 20 minutes.

2. In a separate microwave-safe bowl, combine chocolate chips and ¾ cup (175 mL) of the cream. Microwave on High for 2 minutes, stirring every 30 seconds, until cream is hot and chocolate is shiny and almost melted. Stir until smooth. Whisk until chocolate is completely melted and mixture is smooth.

3. Add remaining cream, milk and sugar to melted chocolate mixture. If mixture is warm, refrigerate or freeze until chilled.

4. Pour mixture into an ice cream maker and freeze according to manufacturer's directions. Without stopping machine, add miniature chocolate chips and raisin mixture when ice cream is thick and almost frozen. Continue freezing until very thick and frozen. Serve immediately or store in freezer for up to 1 day (see Tips, page 119).

Chocolate Cherry Bombs

My daughter thought that these should be called cherry bombs as they have a hidden center of brandied cherries. They have also been proclaimed a "10" on the dessert scale.

Variation
Omit the brandy, if desired.

Baking sheet, lined with waxed paper

6	whole maraschino cherries, drained	6
2 tbsp	brandy	25 mL
2 cups	chocolate ice cream	500 mL
2 cups	semisweet chocolate chips	500 mL
3 tbsp	shortening	45 mL

1. In a small dish, combine cherries and brandy. Set aside for 15 minutes to macerate. Drain cherries and pat dry.

2. Scoop ice cream into six balls, placing on prepared baking sheet. Push a macerated cherry into center of each ice cream ball. Freeze until solid.

3. In a microwave-safe bowl, combine chocolate chips and shortening. Microwave on High for 2 minutes, stirring every 30 seconds, until chocolate is shiny and almost melted. Stir until smooth.

4. Remove ice cream balls from freezer and quickly dip into melted chocolate to coat. Return to pan. Freeze until chocolate is hardened, about 1 hour, or for up to several hours. Serve directly from the freezer.

Chocolate Banana Pops

Remember the chocolate banana pops from county fairs, amusement parks and carnivals? Well, now you don't have to wait for the next time a fair comes through your town to get one. Roll the pops in nuts, candy sprinkles or whatever else strikes your fancy.

Tip
Do not use overripe bananas for this dessert.

Variation
Sprinkle dipped bananas with chopped nuts or candy sprinkles before freezing.

Six wooden Popsicle sticks
Baking sheet, lined with waxed paper

3	large bananas (see Tip, left)	3
2 cups	semisweet chocolate chips	500 mL
3 tbsp	shortening	45 mL

1. Slice bananas in half lengthwise, preferably at an angle. Push a Popsicle stick halfway into cut side of bananas. Place on prepared baking sheet and freeze until frozen solid.

2. In a microwave-safe dish, combine chocolate chips and shortening. Microwave on High for 2 minutes, stirring every 30 seconds, until chocolate is shiny and almost melted. Stir until smooth.

3. Dip frozen bananas into melted chocolate. Return dipped bananas to baking sheet and freeze until chocolate is hardened, about 1 hour. Store in freezer in a resealable freezer bag until ready to serve.

Coconut Chip Sorbet

*This sorbet will transport you
to the Hawaiian Islands. For a
festive touch, you can garnish
it with a sprinkle of toasted
sweetened coconut.*

Tips

Sorbet gets very hard and icy,
so it is best served the day it
is made. However, it can be
frozen for several days in an
airtight container with a piece
of plastic wrap pressed onto
its surface (this prevents the
formation of ice crystals
temporarily). Let the sorbet
sit at room temperature until
soft enough to scoop.

This sorbet is divine with a
drizzle of chocolate sauce.

Variation

Substitute light rum for the
coconut rum.

Ice cream maker

1	can (19 oz/540 mL) unsweetened coconut milk (about $2\frac{1}{2}$ cups/625 mL)	1
$\frac{1}{2}$ cup	superfine sugar	125 mL
$\frac{1}{2}$ cup	water	125 mL
2 tsp	coconut rum	10 mL
$\frac{1}{3}$ cup	miniature semisweet chocolate chips	75 mL

1. In a medium saucepan over medium-high heat, combine coconut milk, sugar and water. Simmer for 5 minutes or until sugar is dissolved. Remove from heat and stir in coconut rum. Pour mixture into a bowl or pitcher and refrigerate until chilled.

2. Pour mixture into ice cream maker and freeze according to manufacturer's directions. When sorbet is thick and almost frozen, add chocolate chips. Continue freezing until very thick and frozen.

3. Serve sorbet immediately or freeze in an airtight container for up to 1 day (see Tips, left).

Frozen Cappuccino

Makes about 5 cups (1.25 L)

One day my mother called to rave about a sorbet she had had. She went on to describe its flavor, aroma and texture. I never got to taste that sorbet, but I developed this one based entirely upon her colorful description. It is truly heavenly.

Tip

This dessert looks great served in espresso cups. Place espresso cups in the freezer for 30 minutes before you're ready to serve the dessert. Remove the cups from the freezer and fill with a scoop of frozen cappuccino. A chocolate chip cookie would make a perfect accompaniment to the sorbet.

Ice cream maker

1 cup	unsweetened Dutch-process cocoa powder, sifted	250 mL
¾ cup	superfine sugar	175 mL
½ tsp	ground cinnamon	2 mL
2 cups	hot freshly brewed coffee	500 mL
½ cup	semisweet chocolate chips	125 mL
½ cup	whipping (35%) cream	125 mL
1 tbsp	gold rum	15 mL
1 tsp	grated orange zest	5 mL
1 tsp	vanilla	5 mL
⅓ cup	miniature semisweet chocolate chips	75 mL

1. In a small bowl, whisk together cocoa powder, sugar and cinnamon.

2. In a large bowl or pitcher, combine hot coffee, chocolate chips, cream, rum, orange zest and vanilla. Whisk in cocoa mixture until smooth.

3. Refrigerate mixture until cold. Pour into ice cream maker and freeze according to manufacturer's directions. When mixture is thick, add miniature chocolate chips. Continue freezing until very thick and frozen.

4. Serve immediately or freeze in an airtight container for up to 1 day (see Tips, page 117).

Tiramisu Chip Gelato

If you are a tiramisu lover, this gelato will blow your socks off. It contains all the luscious flavors you have come to enjoy, but it's frozen.

Tips

The best way to store homemade ice cream is to pack it into a plastic container, press a piece of plastic wrap onto the surface, cover with a tight-fitting plastic lid and freeze. This helps prevent freezer burn.

Be sure to let the frozen ice cream sit at room temperature for a bit to soften slightly before scooping.

Ice cream maker

2 tbsp	coffee liqueur	25 mL
1 tbsp	instant coffee granules	15 mL
1 cup	whipping (35%) cream	250 mL
1	package (8 oz/250 g) cream cheese, softened	1
1/2 cup	superfine sugar	125 mL
1 cup	milk	250 mL
1/2 cup	miniature semisweet chocolate chips	125 mL

1. In a small bowl, stir together coffee liqueur and instant coffee granules.

2. In a food processor fitted with a metal blade, combine cream, cream cheese and sugar. Pulse until smooth, scraping down side of bowl as necessary. Add milk and coffee mixture, pulsing until smooth.

3. Pour into ice cream maker and freeze according to manufacturer's directions. When gelato is thick and almost frozen, add chocolate chips. Continue freezing until very thick and firm.

4. Serve the gelato immediately or freeze in an airtight container for up to 1 day (see Tips, left).

Peppermint Chip Gelato

The flavors in this ice cream are downright refreshing on a hot summer day. The beautiful light pink color brings out the friendly feminine side in each and every one of us. You'll want to start chatting on impact.

Tip

A quick way to chop the candy canes is in a food processor. If you happen to have a mini-processor, it will make the cleanup even easier.

Ice cream maker

1¼ cups	whipping (35%) cream	300 mL
1¼ cups	milk	300 mL
½ cup	superfine sugar	125 mL
½ cup	crushed peppermint candies or candy canes	125 mL
¼ tsp	peppermint extract	1 mL
½ cup	miniature semisweet chocolate chips	125 mL

1. In a bowl, whisk together cream, milk, sugar, crushed peppermint candies and peppermint extract.

2. Pour mixture into ice cream maker and freeze according to manufacturer's directions. When gelato is thick and almost frozen, add chocolate chips. Continue freezing until very thick and firm. Homemade ice cream will be somewhat softer in texture than store-bought.

3. Serve ice cream immediately or freeze in an airtight container for up to 1 day (see Tips, page 119).

Raspberry Chocolate Chip Sorbet

Need a little change in your life? Raspberry, chocolate, wine and lemon blended together and frozen into a remarkable sorbet will cleanse your palate, leaving you feeling fresh and rejuvenated.

Ice cream maker

12 oz	frozen unsweetened raspberries, thawed and including juice (about 3 cups/750 mL)	375 g
1½ cups	water	375 mL
½ cup	superfine sugar	125 mL
2 tbsp	Merlot wine	25 mL
2 tbsp	light corn syrup	25 mL
2 tsp	grated lemon zest	10 mL
⅓ cup	miniature semisweet chocolate chips	75 mL

1. In a food processor fitted with a metal blade, combine thawed raspberries and water. Process until smooth. Strain mixture into a bowl, discarding seeds. Whisk in sugar, wine, corn syrup and lemon zest.

2. Pour mixture into ice cream maker and freeze according to manufacturer's directions. When sorbet is thick and almost frozen, add chocolate chips. Continue freezing until very thick and frozen.

3. Serve the sorbet immediately or freeze in an airtight container for up to 1 day (see Tips, page 117).

Mississippi Mud Pie

Serves 8

Ice cream pies were all the rage in the '60s and '70s. I thought it was about time for a comeback with a contemporary chocolate chip twist.

Variation

Substitute cookies and cream or mint chip ice cream for the coffee ice cream. If using mint chip ice cream, use fudge sauce, not caramel.

9-inch (23 cm) pie plate, greased

20	cream-filled chocolate sandwich cookies	20
1/4 cup	unsalted butter, melted	50 mL
4 cups	coffee ice cream, softened and divided	1 L
1 cup	chocolate fudge or caramel sauce	250 mL
1 cup	semisweet chocolate chips	250 mL
1 1/2 cups	whipping (35%) cream	375 mL
3 tbsp	confectioner's (icing) sugar, sifted	45 mL
1/2 tsp	vanilla	2 mL
1/3 cup	almonds, toasted and coarsely chopped (see Tips, page 33)	75 mL

1. In a food processor fitted with a metal blade, process chocolate sandwich cookies until crumbs form. Add melted butter and process until finely ground. Press mixture into bottom and up side of prepared pie plate. Freeze for 30 minutes or until firm.

2. Spread half of the coffee ice cream over prepared crust. Drizzle evenly with fudge sauce and sprinkle with chocolate chips. Freeze until ice cream hardens slightly. Keep remaining ice cream in the freezer for about 15 minutes, just until the fudge firms up slightly (so that it doesn't ooze into the next ice cream layer). Spread with remaining ice cream.

3. In a bowl, using an electric mixer, combine cream, confectioner's sugar and vanilla. Beat until stiff peaks form.

4. Spread whipped cream over pie and sprinkle with chopped almonds. Freeze for several hours or until completely frozen, or for up to 1 day. If leaving for a day, cover with plastic wrap once it is completely frozen. Let stand at room temperature for 15 minutes before slicing.

Chocolate Chip Dream Cream

This honey-and-cream combo is what dreams are made of. Better REMs are achieved with the addition of chocolate chips! Wake me up before it's all gone.

Variation

For a vanilla version, omit the honey and substitute $1/2$ cup (125 mL) superfine sugar and 2 tsp (10 mL) vanilla.

Ice cream maker

$1\frac{1}{2}$ cups	whipping (35%) cream	375 mL
$1\frac{1}{2}$ cups	milk	375 mL
$1/2$ cup	liquid honey	125 mL
$1/2$ cup	miniature semisweet chocolate chips	125 mL

1. In a bowl, whisk together cream, milk and honey.

2. Pour mixture into ice cream maker and freeze according to manufacturer's directions. When ice cream is thick and almost frozen, add chocolate chips. Continue freezing until very thick and frozen.

3. Serve ice cream immediately or freeze in an airtight container for up to 1 day (see Tips, page 119).

Muffins

Apricot Chocolate Chip Cheesecake Muffins

Makes 12 muffins

I was trying to develop a recipe for a deliciously different muffin, which is how this one was born. It has a chocolate chip cream cheese filling, which is an unexpected surprise.

Preheat oven to 375°F (190°C)
Muffin pan, greased or lined with paper liners

2 cups	all-purpose flour	500 mL
1/2 cup	finely chopped dried apricots	125 mL
2 tsp	baking powder	10 mL
1/4 tsp	salt	1 mL
3/4 cup	granulated sugar	175 mL
2	eggs	2
3/4 cup	milk	175 mL
1/2 cup	vegetable oil	125 mL
1 tsp	vanilla	5 mL
Filling		
3 oz	cream cheese, at room temperature	90 g
3 tbsp	granulated sugar	45 mL
1/8 tsp	almond extract	0.5 mL
1/3 cup	semisweet chocolate chips	75 mL
Topping		
2 tbsp	granulated sugar	25 mL
1/2 tsp	ground cinnamon	2 mL

1. In a medium bowl, combine flour, apricots, baking powder and salt.

2. In a large bowl, whisk together sugar, eggs, milk, oil and vanilla. Stir in flour mixture, mixing just until combined. Do not overmix.

3. *Filling:* In a medium bowl, using electric mixer, beat together cream cheese, sugar and almond extract. Mix in chocolate chips. Set aside.

4. *Topping:* In a small bowl, combine sugar and cinnamon. Set aside.

5. Spoon batter into prepared muffin cups, filling halfway. Drop 1 tsp (5 mL) filling onto center of batter in each muffin cup. Top with more batter. Sprinkle evenly with cinnamon-sugar topping.

6. Bake in preheated oven for 22 to 24 minutes or until puffed, golden and a tester inserted into center comes out clean. Let cool in pan on rack for 5 minutes. Remove from pan and let cool completely on rack.

Almond Poppy Seed Chocolate Chip Muffins

These muffins have a great combination of flavors and the added crunch of almonds, poppy seeds and chocolate chips. For a charming way to serve muffins, line a basket with a beautiful cloth napkin and fill with fresh-baked muffins.

Preheat oven to 375°F (190°C)
Muffin pan, greased or lined with paper liners

2 cups	all-purpose flour	500 mL
3/4 cup	semisweet chocolate chips	175 mL
1 1/2 tbsp	poppy seeds	22 mL
2 tsp	baking powder	10 mL
1/4 tsp	salt	1 mL
1 1/4 cups	granulated sugar, divided	300 mL
2	eggs	2
3/4 cup	milk	175 mL
1/2 cup	vegetable oil	125 mL
2 tsp	almond extract	10 mL
1/4 cup	sliced almonds	50 mL

1. In a medium bowl, combine flour, chocolate chips, poppy seeds, baking powder and salt.

2. In a large bowl, whisk together 1 cup (250 mL) of the sugar, eggs, milk, oil and almond extract. Stir in flour mixture, mixing just until combined. Do not overmix.

3. Spoon batter into prepared muffin cups. Sprinkle remaining sugar and sliced almonds evenly over tops.

4. Bake in preheated oven for 20 to 24 minutes or until puffed, golden and a tester inserted into center comes out clean. Let cool in pan on rack for 5 minutes. Remove from pan and let cool completely on rack.

Old-Fashioned Dark Chocolate Pudding *(page 160)*
and Chocolate Cherry Biscotti *(page 88)*

Overleaf: Frozen Cappuccino *(page 118)*

Chocolate Chip Cranberry Muffins

This is a great muffin, especially if you're a cranberry fan. The delightful tartness of the cranberries wedded with the sweetness of the chocolate chips makes for a very yummy treat.

Preheat oven to 375°F (190°C)
Muffin pan, greased or lined with paper liners

2 cups	all-purpose flour	500 mL
2 tsp	baking powder	10 mL
1/4 tsp	salt	1 mL
1 1/2 cups	fresh or frozen cranberries	375 mL
1 1/4 cups	granulated sugar, divided	300 mL
2	eggs	2
3/4 cup	milk	175 mL
1/2 cup	vegetable oil	125 mL
1 tsp	grated orange zest	5 mL
1 tsp	vanilla	5 mL
1/2 cup	semisweet chocolate chips	125 mL

1. In a medium bowl, combine flour, baking powder and salt.

2. In a food processor fitted with a metal blade, coarsely chop cranberries.

3. In a large bowl, whisk together 1 cup (250 mL) of the sugar, eggs, milk, oil, orange zest and vanilla. Stir in flour mixture, just until combined. Fold in chopped cranberries and chocolate chips. Do not overmix.

4. Spoon batter into prepared muffin cups. Sprinkle evenly with remaining sugar.

5. Bake in preheated oven for 20 to 24 minutes or until puffed, golden and a tester inserted into center comes out clean. Let cool in pan on rack for 5 minutes. Remove from pan and let cool completely on rack.

Chocolate Tiramisu *(page 163)*

Chocolate Chip Eggnog Muffins

This is a great seasonal muffin. Eggnog is usually available from October through January. The creamy nutmeg flavor always makes me think of winter.

Preheat oven to 375°F (190°C)
Muffin pan, greased or lined with paper liners

2 cups	all-purpose flour	500 mL
¾ cup	semisweet chocolate chips	175 mL
2 tsp	baking powder	10 mL
1 tsp	grated nutmeg	5 mL
¼ tsp	salt	1 mL
1 cup	granulated sugar, divided	250 mL
2	eggs	2
¾ cup	eggnog (not low-fat)	175 mL
½ cup	vegetable oil	125 mL

1. In a medium bowl, combine flour, chocolate chips, baking powder, nutmeg and salt.

2. In a large bowl, whisk together ¾ cup (175 mL) of the sugar, eggs, eggnog and oil. Stir in flour mixture just until combined. Do not overmix.

3. Spoon batter into prepared muffin cups. Sprinkle evenly with remaining sugar.

4. Bake in preheated oven for 20 to 24 minutes or until puffed, golden and a tester inserted into center comes out clean. Let cool in pan on rack for 5 minutes. Remove from pan and let cool completely on rack.

Chocolate Chip Orange Muffins

I have always thought that the combination of chocolate and orange is a treat for the senses. The two flavors can truly turn something ordinary into something extraordinary! This muffin proves the point.

Preheat oven to 375°F (190°C)
Muffin pan, greased or lined with paper liners

2 cups	all-purpose flour	500 mL
2 tsp	baking powder	10 mL
¼ tsp	salt	1 mL
1¼ cups	granulated sugar, divided	300 mL
2	eggs	2
¾ cup	milk	175 mL
½ cup	vegetable oil	125 mL
2 tsp	grated orange zest	10 mL
1 tsp	vanilla	5 mL
1 tsp	orange extract	5 mL
¾ cup	semisweet chocolate chips	175 mL

1. In a medium bowl, combine flour, baking powder and salt.

2. In a large bowl, whisk together 1 cup (250 mL) of the sugar, eggs, milk, oil, orange zest, vanilla and orange extract. Stir in flour mixture just until combined. Fold in chocolate chips. Do not overmix.

3. Spoon batter into prepared muffin cups. Sprinkle evenly with remaining sugar.

4. Bake in preheated oven for 20 to 24 minutes or until puffed, golden and a tester inserted into center comes out clean. Let cool in pan on rack for 5 minutes. Remove from pan and let cool completely on rack.

Maple Pecan Muffins with Chocolate Chips

If you love the taste of maple and pecan, you will love these muffins. If you can't find pecans, you can easily substitute walnuts.

Preheat oven to 375°F (190°C)
Muffin pan, greased or lined with paper liners

2 cups	all-purpose flour	500 mL
2 tsp	baking powder	10 mL
1/4 tsp	salt	1 mL
2 tbsp	granulated sugar	25 mL
3/4 cup	chopped pecans, divided	175 mL
1/2 cup	unsalted butter, melted	125 mL
3/4 cup	packed light brown sugar	175 mL
2	eggs	2
3/4 cup	milk	175 mL
1 tsp	vanilla	5 mL
1 tsp	maple extract	5 mL
3/4 cup	semisweet chocolate chips	175 mL

1. In a medium bowl, combine flour, baking powder and salt.

2. In a small bowl, combine granulated sugar and half of the pecans. Set aside.

3. In a large bowl, beat butter and brown sugar. Add eggs, one at a time, beating well after each addition. Stir in milk, vanilla and maple extract. Stir in flour mixture just until combined. Fold in chocolate chips and remaining pecans. Do not overmix.

4. Spoon batter into prepared muffin cups. Sprinkle evenly with reserved pecan mixture.

5. Bake in preheated oven for 20 to 24 minutes or until puffed, golden and a tester inserted into center comes out clean. Let cool in pan on rack for 5 minutes. Remove from pan and let cool completely on rack.

Chocolate Chip Pumpkin Muffins

*Pumpkin is high in
beta-carotene, making
these scrumptious muffins
as virtuous as they are
delicious. They are a great
lunch box stuffer or a quick
breakfast on the go.*

Tip

For a less sweet muffin,
reduce the sugar in the batter
to ³⁄₄ cup (175 mL).

Preheat oven to 375°F (190°C)
Muffin pan, greased or lined with paper liners

2 cups	all-purpose flour	500 mL
³⁄₄ cup	semisweet chocolate chips	175 mL
2 tsp	baking powder	10 mL
1¹⁄₂ tsp	ground cinnamon	7 mL
³⁄₄ tsp	ground allspice	4 mL
³⁄₄ tsp	ground nutmeg	4 mL
¹⁄₄ tsp	salt	1 mL
1¹⁄₄ cups	granulated sugar, divided	300 mL
2	eggs	2
³⁄₄ cup	canned pumpkin purée (not pie filling)	175 mL
¹⁄₂ cup	vegetable oil	125 mL
¹⁄₄ cup	milk	50 mL
1 tsp	vanilla	5 mL

1. In a medium bowl, combine flour, chocolate chips, baking powder, cinnamon, allspice, nutmeg and salt.

2. In a large bowl, whisk together 1 cup (250 mL) of the sugar, eggs, pumpkin, oil, milk and vanilla. Stir in flour mixture just until combined. Do not overmix.

3. Spoon batter into prepared muffin cups. Sprinkle evenly with remaining sugar.

4. Bake in preheated oven for 20 to 24 minutes or until puffed, golden and a tester inserted into center comes out clean. Let cool in pan on rack for 5 minutes. Remove from pan and let cool completely on rack.

Crumbcake Muffins

This is a great basic muffin, equally delish with a cup of Joe. Try making this recipe with an assortment of other muffins for a weekend brunch.

Preheat oven to 375°F (190°C)
Muffin pan, greased or lined with paper liners

Topping

½ cup	confectioner's (icing) sugar	125 mL
½ cup	all-purpose flour	125 mL
½ tsp	ground cinnamon	2 mL
⅛ tsp	salt	0.5 mL
¼ cup	unsalted butter, melted	50 mL

Batter

2 cups	all-purpose flour	500 mL
¾ cup	semisweet chocolate chips	175 mL
2 tsp	baking powder	10 mL
¼ tsp	salt	1 mL
¾ cup	granulated sugar	175 mL
2	eggs	2
¾ cup	milk	175 mL
½ cup	vegetable oil	125 mL
1 tsp	vanilla	5 mL
	Ground cinnamon	

1. *Topping:* In a medium bowl, whisk together confectioner's sugar, flour, cinnamon and salt. Pour in melted butter and whisk until crumbly. Set aside.

2. *Batter:* In a medium bowl, combine flour, chocolate chips, baking powder and salt.

3. In a large bowl, whisk together sugar, eggs, milk, oil and vanilla. Stir in flour mixture just until combined. Do not overmix.

4. Spoon batter into prepared muffin cups. Sprinkle evenly with reserved topping, then ground cinnamon.

5. Bake in preheated oven for 22 to 24 minutes or until puffed, golden and a tester inserted into center comes out clean. Let cool in pan on rack for 5 minutes. Remove from pan and let cool completely on rack.

Chocolate Chip Lemon Muffins

This muffin is delish! Lemon and chocolate are always a smashing combo, and here they result in an out-of-sight muffin. My young taste testers were very impressed with these tender little cakes.

Preheat oven to 375°F (190°C)
Muffin pan, greased or lined with paper liners

2 cups	all-purpose flour	500 mL
1¼ cups	granulated sugar, divided	300 mL
2 tsp	baking powder	10 mL
2	eggs	2
¾ cup	milk	175 mL
½ cup	butter, melted	125 mL
2 tsp	grated lemon zest	10 mL
¼ cup	freshly squeezed lemon juice	50 mL
½ cup	semisweet chocolate chips	125 mL

1. In a medium bowl, combine flour, 1 cup (250 mL) of the sugar and baking powder.

2. In a large bowl, whisk together eggs, milk, butter, lemon zest and lemon juice. Stir in flour mixture, mixing just until combined. Fold in chocolate chips. Do not overmix.

3. Scoop batter into prepared muffin cups. Sprinkle remaining sugar evenly over tops.

4. Bake in preheated oven for 20 to 24 minutes or until puffed, light golden and a skewer inserted into center comes out clean. Let cool in pan on rack for 5 minutes. Remove from pan and let cool completely on rack.

Donut Muffins

Caution: These buttery treats will disappear fast. You might need to make a double batch. The nutmeg-scented muffins are dipped in melted butter, then rolled in cinnamon sugar.

Preheat oven to 350°F (180°C)
Muffin pan, greased or lined with paper liners

1½ cups	all-purpose flour	375 mL
1½ tsp	baking powder	7 mL
¼ tsp	ground nutmeg	1 mL
¼ tsp	salt	1 mL
½ cup	unsalted butter, at room temperature	125 mL
½ cup	granulated sugar	125 mL
1	egg	1
½ cup	milk	125 mL
½ cup	semisweet chocolate chips	125 mL

Topping

½ cup	granulated sugar	125 mL
1 tsp	ground cinnamon	5 mL
½ cup	unsalted butter, melted	125 mL

1. In a medium bowl, combine flour, baking powder, nutmeg and salt.

2. In a large bowl, using electric mixer, beat butter and sugar until light and fluffy. Beat in egg. Beat in flour mixture alternately with milk, making three additions of flour mixture and two of milk. Do not overmix. Stir in chocolate chips.

3. Spoon batter into prepared muffin cups. Bake in preheated oven for 20 to 22 minutes or until puffed, golden and a tester inserted into center comes out clean. Let cool in pan on rack for 5 minutes. Remove from pan and let cool completely on rack.

4. *Topping:* In a bowl, combine sugar and cinnamon. Place melted butter in another bowl. Dip warm muffins in melted butter, then roll in cinnamon-sugar topping. Serve warm or let cool on rack.

Double Chocolate Chip Muffins

A cross between a brownie and chocolate cake, these muffins are a chocoholic's dream, delivering a double dose of chocolate in every bite.

Preheat oven to 375°F (190°C)
Muffin pan, greased or lined with paper liners

1¾ cups	all-purpose flour	425 mL
½ cup	unsweetened Dutch-process cocoa powder, sifted	125 mL
2 tsp	baking powder	10 mL
¼ tsp	salt	1 mL
1½ cups	granulated sugar, divided	375 mL
2	eggs	2
¾ cup	milk	175 mL
½ cup	vegetable oil	125 mL
2 tsp	vanilla	10 mL
1 cup	semisweet chocolate chips	250 mL

1. In a medium bowl, combine flour, cocoa powder, baking powder and salt.

2. In a large bowl, whisk together 1 cup (250 mL) of the sugar, eggs, milk, oil and vanilla. Stir in flour mixture just until combined. Fold in chocolate chips. Do not overmix.

3. Spoon batter into prepared muffin cups. Sprinkle evenly with remaining sugar.

4. Bake in preheated oven for 22 minutes or until puffed and a tester inserted into center comes out clean. Let cool in pan on rack for 5 minutes. Remove from pan and let cool completely on rack.

Ginger Muffins

Makes 12 muffins

Crystallized or candied ginger almost tickles the funny bone, awakening the senses as you eat it. The best part is that it can be found in most supermarkets these days. It has a long shelf life, if stored in an airtight jar or container.

Preheat oven to 375°F (190°C)
Muffin pan, greased or lined with paper liners

2 cups	all-purpose flour	500 mL
1 tbsp plus 2 tsp	ground ginger	25 mL
2 tsp	baking powder	10 mL
1 tsp	ground allspice	5 mL
1/4 tsp	salt	1 mL
1/4 tsp	ground nutmeg	1 mL
1 cup	granulated sugar, divided	250 mL
1/3 cup	packed dark brown sugar	75 mL
2	eggs	2
2/3 cup	milk	150 mL
1/2 cup	vegetable oil	125 mL
1/4 cup	fancy molasses	50 mL
3/4 cup	semisweet chocolate chips	175 mL
1/4 cup	finely chopped crystallized ginger	50 mL

1. In a medium bowl, combine flour, ginger, baking powder, allspice, salt and nutmeg.

2. In a large bowl, whisk together 3/4 cup (175 mL) of the granulated sugar, brown sugar, eggs, milk, oil and molasses. Stir in flour mixture just until combined. Fold in chocolate chips. Do not overmix.

3. Spoon batter into prepared muffin cups. Sprinkle evenly with remaining sugar and crystallized ginger.

4. Bake in preheated oven for 22 minutes or until puffed, golden and a tester inserted into center comes out clean. Let cool in pan on rack for 5 minutes. Remove from pan and let cool completely on rack.

High-Octane Espresso Chip Morning Muffins

When my family and I were in Victoria, British Columbia, on a road trip, we stopped by a fabulous little bakeshop, Cascadia Wholefoods Bakery. My son devoured one of the delicious coffee muffins, immediately giving me the orders to recreate them upon our return. This is my version.

Preheat oven to 350°F (180°C)
Muffin pan, greased or lined with paper liners

2 cups	all-purpose flour	500 mL
2 tsp	baking powder	10 mL
1 tsp	ground cinnamon	5 mL
1/4 tsp	salt	1 mL
1 cup	granulated sugar	250 mL
2	eggs	2
3/4 cup	milk	175 mL
1/2 cup	vegetable oil	125 mL
2 tbsp	finely ground espresso	25 mL
1 1/2 tbsp	instant coffee granules	22 mL
1 tsp	vanilla	5 mL
3/4 cup	semisweet chocolate chips	175 mL

Topping

2 tbsp	granulated sugar	25 mL
1/2 tsp	ground cinnamon	2 mL

1. In a medium bowl, combine flour, baking powder, cinnamon and salt.

2. In a large bowl, whisk together sugar, eggs, milk, oil, finely ground and instant coffees and vanilla. Stir in flour mixture just until combined. Fold in chocolate chips. Do not overmix.

3. *Topping:* In a small bowl, combine sugar and cinnamon. Set aside.

4. Spoon batter into prepared muffin cups. Sprinkle evenly with cinnamon-sugar topping.

5. Bake in preheated oven for 20 to 22 minutes or until puffed, firm to the touch and a tester inserted into center comes out clean. Let cool in pan on rack for 5 minutes. Remove from pan and let cool completely on rack.

Raspberry Chocolate Chip Muffins

Fresh or frozen raspberries make this easy-to-prepare recipe a favorite in my household. The tart raspberries, sweet chocolate chips and delicate batter are a perfect combination to wake up the taste buds.

Preheat oven to 375°F (190°C)
Muffin pan, greased or lined with paper liners

2 cups	all-purpose flour	500 mL
2 tsp	baking powder	10 mL
1/4 tsp	salt	1 mL
1 1/4 cups	granulated sugar, divided	300 mL
2	eggs	2
3/4 cup	milk	175 mL
1/2 cup	vegetable oil	125 mL
1 tsp	almond extract	5 mL
2 cups	raspberries, fresh or frozen (do not thaw)	500 mL
1/2 cup	semisweet chocolate chips	125 mL

1. In a medium bowl, combine flour, baking powder and salt.

2. In a large bowl, whisk together 1 cup (250 mL) of the sugar, eggs, milk, oil and almond extract. Stir in flour mixture just until combined. Fold in raspberries and chocolate chips. Do not overmix.

3. Spoon batter into prepared muffin cups. Sprinkle evenly with remaining sugar.

4. Bake in preheated oven for 22 to 25 minutes or until puffed, golden and a tester inserted into center comes out clean. Let cool in pan on rack for 5 minutes. Remove from pan and let cool completely on rack.

Sour Cream Coffee Cake Muffins

This is an ideal recipe when you have a craving for coffee cake but don't have the time to make it. The rich, tender batter is the perfect partner for the tasty chocolate chip walnut topping.

Preheat oven to 375°F (190°C)
Muffin pan, greased or lined with paper liners

2 cups	all-purpose flour	500 mL
2 tsp	baking powder	10 mL
1/4 tsp	salt	1 mL
1/2 cup	unsalted butter, at room temperature	125 mL
1 cup	granulated sugar	250 mL
1 tsp	vanilla	5 mL
2	eggs	2
1 cup	sour cream	250 mL

Topping

1/2 cup	granulated sugar	125 mL
1/2 cup	coarsely chopped walnuts	125 mL
1/2 cup	semisweet chocolate chips	125 mL
1 tsp	ground cinnamon	5 mL

1. In a medium bowl, combine flour, baking powder and salt.

2. In a bowl, using electric mixer, beat butter and sugar until light and fluffy. Beat in vanilla. Add eggs, one at a time, beating well after each addition. Add sour cream and beat until smooth. Add flour mixture and beat just until combined.

3. *Topping:* In a medium bowl, combine sugar, walnuts, chocolate chips and cinnamon. Spoon batter into prepared muffin cups, filling halfway. Sprinkle evenly with half of the topping. Spoon in remaining batter and sprinkle with remaining topping.

4. Bake in preheated oven for 24 minutes or until puffed, golden and a tester inserted into center comes out clean. Let cool in pan on rack for 5 minutes. Remove from pan and let cool completely on rack.

Strawberry Chocolate Chip Muffins

This light cornmeal batter is the perfect housing for the strawberry and chocolate chip filling. Don't worry if there is filling left over. Save it and spread it on warm toast for breakfast.

Tip

To give the muffin tops a sparkly appearance, sprinkle lightly with sugar.

Preheat oven to 375°F (190°C)
Muffin pan, greased or lined with paper liners

Filling

1/3 cup	semisweet chocolate chips	75 mL
1/4 cup	strawberry jam	50 mL

Batter

1 3/4 cups	all-purpose flour	425 mL
3/4 cup	cornmeal	175 mL
2 tsp	baking powder	10 mL
1/4 tsp	salt	1 mL
1 cup	sour cream	250 mL
1/2 cup	granulated sugar	125 mL
1/2 cup	unsalted butter, melted and cooled	125 mL
2	eggs	2

1. *Filling:* In a small bowl, combine chocolate chips and strawberry jam. Set aside.

2. *Batter:* In a medium bowl, combine flour, cornmeal, baking powder and salt.

3. In a large bowl, whisk together sour cream, sugar, melted butter and eggs until smooth. Stir in flour mixture just until combined.

4. Spoon batter into prepared muffin cups. Using a spoon, make an indentation in center of each. Fill indentations with a scant teaspoon (5 mL) of the filling.

5. Bake in preheated oven for 22 to 24 minutes or until puffed, golden and a tester inserted into center comes out clean. Let cool in pan on rack for 5 minutes. Remove from pan and let cool completely on rack.

Pies and Tarts

Almond and Coconut Chocolate Chip Tart

This elegant and delicious tart is an adaptation of a recipe that I developed for Bon Appetit Magazine. It is also a fabulous dessert for a dinner party, as you can make the entire dessert ahead of time.

Tip

Garnish the tart with a light dusting of confectioner's (icing) sugar, if desired.

Preheat oven to 350°F (180°C)
11-inch (28 cm) metal tart pan with removable bottom, greased

1½ cups	all-purpose flour	375 mL
¼ cup	granulated sugar	50 mL
½ cup	unsalted butter, chilled and cut into pieces	125 mL
2 tbsp	whipping (35%) cream	25 mL
1½ tsp	vanilla	7 mL

Filling

¾ cup	light corn syrup	175 mL
¼ cup	packed light brown sugar	50 mL
¼ cup	butter, melted and cooled	50 mL
3	eggs	3
1 tsp	vanilla	5 mL
2 cups	whole almonds, toasted and coarsely chopped (see Tips, page 33)	500 mL
1 cup	semisweet chocolate chips	250 mL
½ cup	sweetened flaked coconut	125 mL

1. In a food processor fitted with a metal blade, combine flour and sugar. Pulse to combine. Add butter and pulse just until mixture resembles coarse meal. Add cream and vanilla, pulsing just until moist clumps form. If dough is dry, add more cream, 1 tbsp (15 mL) at a time. Pulse again, just until dough starts to form a ball. Press into prepared pan.

2. *Filling:* In a large bowl, whisk together corn syrup, brown sugar and melted butter. Whisk in eggs and vanilla. Mix in almonds, chocolate chips and coconut. Pour filling over prepared crust.

3. Bake in preheated oven for 50 minutes or until tart is firmly set in center and top is golden brown.

4. Let tart cool in pan on rack. Push up bottom of pan to release. Serve tart warm or at room temperature.

Chocolate Chip Brownie Tart

This delicious tart will keep, refrigerated, for several days. For such a humble dessert, it has a sophisticated look to it. Serve it with a scoop of your favorite premium ice cream.

Preheat oven to 325°F (160°C)
10-inch (25 cm) glass tart dish or quiche dish, greased

1/3 cup	all-purpose flour	75 mL
1/8 tsp	salt	0.5 mL
4 oz	unsweetened chocolate, chopped	125 g
1/2 cup	unsalted butter	125 mL
1 1/4 cups	packed light brown sugar	300 mL
2	eggs	2
1 tsp	vanilla	5 mL
1/2 cup	semisweet chocolate chips	125 mL

1. In a small bowl, mix together flour and salt. Set aside.

2. In a large microwave-safe bowl, combine unsweetened chocolate and butter. Microwave on High for 2 to 2 1/2 minutes, stirring every 30 seconds, until butter is melted and chocolate is shiny and almost melted. Stir until smooth. Let cool to lukewarm. Whisk in sugar, eggs and vanilla. Stir in flour mixture just until combined.

3. Spread in prepared dish. Sprinkle with chocolate chips. Bake in preheated oven for 30 to 35 minutes or until a toothpick inserted into center comes out clean. Let cool in dish on rack. Cover and refrigerate for several hours or until firm, or overnight.

Banana Fanna Pie

My friend Erika Novick and I used to make banana cream pies together all the time. I've added chocolate chips to our original recipe — taking it from fabulous to oh so fabulous.

Variation

Whisk ³/₄ cup (175 mL) semisweet chocolate chips into hot custard mixture for a double chocolate banana pie.

Preheat oven to 400°F (200°C)

1	unbaked 9-inch (23 cm) pie shell (frozen or homemade)	1
³/₄ cup	semisweet chocolate chips, divided	175 mL
1 cup plus 2 tbsp	whipping (35%) cream, divided	275 mL
3	egg yolks	3
³/₄ cup	granulated sugar	175 mL
¹/₄ cup	all-purpose flour	50 mL
¹/₄ cup	cornstarch	50 mL
¹/₈ tsp	salt	0.5 mL
3 cups	half-and-half (10%) cream, divided	750 mL
2 tbsp	unsalted butter	25 mL
1 tbsp	confectioner's (icing) sugar, sifted	15 mL
¹/₄ tsp	vanilla	1 mL
2	medium bananas, sliced	2

1. If frozen, let pie shell thaw for 10 minutes. Place on a baking sheet. Lightly prick bottom and sides of shell with a fork (be careful not to make large holes). Bake in preheated oven until crust is lightly browned, 13 to 15 minutes. Let cool completely on rack.

2. In a microwave-safe bowl, combine ¹/₂ cup (125 mL) of the chocolate chips and 2 tbsp (25 mL) of the whipping cream. Microwave on High for 1 to 2 minutes, stirring every 30 seconds, until chocolate is shiny and almost melted. Stir until smooth. Spread chocolate mixture over bottom of cooled crust. Refrigerate until chocolate is firm.

3. Meanwhile, in a small bowl, whisk together egg yolks, granulated sugar, flour, cornstarch and salt. Whisk in $\frac{1}{2}$ cup (125 mL) of the half-and-half until smooth.

4. In a large saucepan, bring remaining half-and-half to boil over medium-high heat. Remove saucepan from heat and gradually whisk in egg yolk mixture. Reduce heat to medium and return pan to stovetop. Cook, whisking constantly, until thick and smooth, 3 to 4 minutes. Whisk in butter. Pour custard into a bowl and place a sheet of plastic wrap directly on surface to prevent a skin from forming. Let cool completely.

5. In a bowl, using electric mixer or whisk, whip remaining whipping cream, confectioner's sugar and vanilla until stiff peaks form.

6. Layer banana slices over chocolate in crust. Spoon cooled custard over bananas. Top pie with whipped cream and sprinkle with remaining chocolate chips. Chill for several hours or until firm before serving.

Chocolate Chip Cheese Tart

This is similar to a cheesecake but better. It goes together quickly and looks impressive. The chocolate drizzle on top gives it a striking appearance.

Variation

Substitute light rum for the coconut rum.

9-inch (23 cm) tart pan with removable bottom, sprayed with nonstick spray

10	whole graham crackers	10
5 tbsp	unsalted butter, melted	75 mL
1/3 cup	sweetened flaked coconut	75 mL
12 oz	cream cheese, softened	375 g
1/2 cup	superfine sugar	125 mL
1 3/4 cups	whipping (35%) cream	425 mL
2 1/2 tbsp	coconut rum	32 mL
1/2 cup	semisweet chocolate chips	125 mL
1 1/2 tsp	shortening	7 mL
1/3 cup	miniature semisweet chocolate chips	75 mL

1. In a food processor fitted with a metal blade, pulse graham crackers until fine crumbs form. Transfer crumbs to a medium bowl. Stir in melted butter and coconut. Press into bottom and up side of prepared tart pan. Freeze until firm.

2. In a bowl, using electric mixer, combine cream cheese and sugar. Whip until creamy, scraping down side of bowl as necessary. Add cream and rum, whipping until mixture looks like whipped cream and soft peaks form.

3. Spread whipped cream mixture over frozen crust, using back of spoon to swirl decoratively.

4. In a microwave-safe bowl, combine 1/2 cup (125 mL) chocolate chips and shortening. Microwave on High for 1 to 2 minutes, stirring every 30 seconds, until chocolate is shiny and almost melted. Stir until smooth.

5. Drizzle melted chocolate over top of cheese mixture. Sprinkle with miniature chocolate chips. Refrigerate for several hours or until firm, or for up to 8 hours. (If left any longer, the crust will get soggy.)

Chocolate Chip Coconut Pie

This dessert — a chewy, ooey-gooey chocolate chip cookie baked in a flaky pastry crust — acts like a party in your mouth.

Tip

Serve a slice of pie with a scoop of vanilla ice cream.

Variation

Substitute walnuts for the coconut.

Preheat oven to 350°F (180°C)

1 cup	granulated sugar	250 mL
1 cup	semisweet chocolate chips	250 mL
1/2 cup	all-purpose flour	125 mL
1/2 cup	sweetened flaked coconut	125 mL
1/8 tsp	salt	0.5 mL
1/2 cup	unsalted butter, melted and cooled slightly	125 mL
2	eggs	2
1 tsp	vanilla	5 mL
1	unbaked 9-inch (23 cm) deep-dish pie shell (frozen or homemade)	1
	Confectioner's (icing) sugar, for garnish	

1. In a large bowl, combine sugar, chocolate chips, flour, coconut and salt. Add melted butter, eggs and vanilla, stirring well.

2. Pour mixture into pie shell. Bake in preheated oven for 45 minutes or until a knife inserted into center comes out almost clean. Let cool completely on rack.

3. Lightly dust the top of the cooled pie with confectioner's sugar.

Chocolate Chip Pecan Pie

For Thanksgiving, I was busy baking chocolate chip pecan pies but could not get them to set. Our friend Rick, who is from New Orleans, suggested that I follow the recipe he uses for pecan pie: the one on the back of the corn syrup bottle. This is my version of Rick's favorite recipe.

Variation

Substitute walnuts for the pecans.

Preheat oven to 350°F (180°C)

3	eggs	3
³⁄₄ cup	firmly packed dark brown sugar	175 mL
1 cup	light corn syrup	250 mL
2 tbsp	unsalted butter, melted and cooled slightly	25 mL
1 tsp	vanilla	5 mL
⅛ tsp	salt	0.5 mL
⅓ cup	semisweet chocolate chips	75 mL
1⅓ cups	pecans, toasted (see Tip, page 83)	325 mL
1	unbaked 9-inch (23 cm) deep-dish pie shell (frozen or homemade)	1

1. In a large bowl, whisk eggs. Add brown sugar, corn syrup, melted butter, vanilla and salt, whisking well. Stir in chocolate chips.

2. Place pecans in bottom of pie shell. Pour filling over top. Bake in preheated oven for 50 to 55 minutes or until a knife inserted into center of pie comes out clean. Let cool completely on rack.

Chocolate Chip Mocha Tarts

*I usually have a roll or two
of homemade chocolate chip
cookie dough in my freezer.
I have found it makes great
tart crust for recipes like this.
It is a fun recipe to make with
kids as they find the tarts not
only delicious but "fancy" too.*

Tip

The large cookie tarts take
12 to 14 minutes to bake.
You can also freeze the
cooled filled tarts. Just be
sure to store them in a
resealable freezer bag.

Preheat oven to 350°F (180°C)
Mini muffin tins or standard-size muffin tin, greased

1 lb	log chocolate chip cookie dough (see Slice-and-Bake Chocolate Chip Almond Cookies, page 106, with or without the almonds), or store-bought cookie dough	500 g
1 pint	coffee ice cream	500 mL
	Miniature semisweet chocolate chips	
	Whipped (35%) cream or fudge sauce (optional)	

1. Remove cookie dough from freezer or refrigerator (if frozen, let stand at room temperature until slightly softened). Cut dough into $1/4$-inch (0.5 cm) thick slices and press into prepared muffin cups. Bake tarts in preheated oven for 10 minutes or until puffed and golden brown. Let cool in tins on rack for 5 minutes. Remove from tins and let cool completely on rack.

2. Place a scoop of ice cream on top of each cookie tart. Sprinkle with miniature chocolate chips. Garnish with whipped cream, if desired. Serve immediately.

Old-Fashioned Chocolate Orange Pie

Don't let the name fool you. This dessert is a favorite with all ages. The chocolate orange flavor lends an air of sophistication to an old-fashioned pie.

Tip

You will find it easiest to cook this pudding in a heavy-bottomed nonstick saucepan.

Variation

For a pure chocolate variation, substitute ½ cup (125 mL) milk for the orange juice and omit the orange zest.

¼ cup	granulated sugar	50 mL
2 tbsp	all-purpose flour	25 mL
2 tbsp	cornstarch	25 mL
⅛ tsp	salt	0.5 mL
1½ cups	milk, divided	375 mL
2	egg yolks	2
1 tsp	grated orange zest	5 mL
½ cup	orange juice	125 mL
1 cup	semisweet chocolate chips	250 mL
1 tbsp	unsalted butter	15 mL
½ tsp	vanilla	2 mL
1	9-inch (23 cm) pie shell, baked and cooled	1
1 cup	whipping (35%) cream	250 mL
1 tbsp	confectioner's (icing) sugar	15 mL
½ tsp	vanilla	2 mL
	Semisweet chocolate chips, for garnish (optional)	

1. In a medium bowl, whisk together sugar, flour, cornstarch and salt. Whisk in ½ cup (125 mL) of the milk and egg yolks. Set aside.

2. In a large saucepan over medium-high heat, bring remaining milk, orange zest and juice to a simmer, whisking often (don't worry if it starts to curdle). Remove saucepan from heat and whisk in egg yolk mixture. Reduce heat to medium, return saucepan to burner and cook, whisking constantly, until thickened. Remove from heat and whisk in chocolate chips, butter and vanilla until smooth. Let cool slightly. Pour into cooled pie crust.

3. In a medium bowl, with electric mixer or whisk, whip together cream, confectioner's sugar and vanilla until almost stiff peaks. Swirl top of pie with whipped cream and sprinkle with additional chocolate chips, if desired. Chill for several hours before serving.

Puddings

Better-Than-Store-Bought Chocolate Pudding Mix

Makes about 8 cups (2 L) pudding mix

When I was growing up, my mother would always have a big container of homemade pudding mix on hand. It is amazing how simple and quick it is to put this together. Plus, there aren't any preservatives, colors or other additives in this mix.

Serves 2 to 4

Tip

When making the pudding with this mix, the recipe can be doubled.

Variations

Sprinkle a little ground cinnamon into the warm pudding.

For a richer taste, whisk 1 tbsp (15 mL) butter into hot pudding.

Pudding Mix

4 cups	nonfat dry milk	1 L
1¾ cups	granulated sugar	425 mL
1½ cups	unsweetened Dutch-process cocoa powder, sifted	375 mL
1½ cups	cornstarch	375 mL
¾ tsp	salt	4 mL
2 cups	semisweet chocolate chips	500 mL

Pudding

2 cups	milk, divided	500 mL
1 cup	pudding mix	250 mL
½ tsp	vanilla	2 mL

1. *Pudding Mix:* In a large bowl, whisk together dry milk, sugar, cocoa powder, cornstarch and salt. Stir in chocolate chips.

2. Transfer to an airtight container or glass jar. Store at room temperature for up to 6 months.

3. *Pudding:* In a bowl, whisk ½ cup (125 mL) of the milk with pudding mix. Set aside. In a medium saucepan, heat remaining milk until steaming and very warm to the touch. Gradually whisk in pudding mixture. Cook, whisking constantly, until thickened and bubbling.

4. Remove from heat and stir in vanilla. Pour pudding into a serving bowl or scoop into individual dessert bowls. Let stand for 15 minutes before serving. Alternatively, cover and refrigerate cooled pudding and serve chilled.

Chocolate Chip Bread Pudding with Irish Cream

Irish Cream makes an unbelievably delicious bread pudding. My friend Susan Bussel proclaimed this dessert a "10." I just know that once I start eating this pudding, I can't stop. It's comfort food at its best!

Preheat oven to 350°F (180°C), with rack placed in center of oven

13-by 9-inch (3 L) baking dish, greased

8 cups	loosely packed bread cubes (preferably egg bread)	2 L
9	eggs	9
3⅓ cups	milk	825 mL
1 cup	whipping (35%) cream	250 mL
¾ cup	packed light brown sugar	175 mL
¾ cup	granulated sugar	175 mL
½ cup	Irish Cream liqueur	125 mL
1 cup	semisweet chocolate chips	250 mL

1. Place bread cubes in prepared dish. Set aside.

2. In a large bowl, whisk eggs well. Whisk in milk, cream, brown sugar, granulated sugar and liqueur. Pour mixture over bread cubes and let stand for 10 minutes so that bread absorbs liquid. With a spatula, press down bread cubes into liquid once or twice. Sprinkle chocolate chips over top, pressing them in with a fork.

3. Bake in preheated oven until custard is set but still slightly wobbly in the center, about 45 minutes. Let cool on a rack.

Chocolate Banana Bread Pudding

Being a huge fan of chocolate and banana, I love the flavors in this bread pudding. The bananas almost have a roasted flavor, which is divine in this not-so-traditional pudding.

Tip

Serve this dessert warm with a scoop of vanilla ice cream, if desired.

Preheat oven to 350°F (180°C)
8-inch (2 L) square glass baking dish, greased

4½ cups	loosely packed bread cubes	1.125 L
1½	medium bananas, sliced ¼ inch (0.5 cm) thick	1½
⅓ cup	semisweet chocolate chips	75 mL
3	eggs	3
2	egg yolks	2
¾ cup	packed light brown sugar	175 mL
2½ cups	milk	625 mL
1 tsp	vanilla	5 mL
2 tbsp	bourbon (optional)	25 mL

1. Place bread cubes in prepared dish. Scatter banana slices over top. Sprinkle with chocolate chips.

2. In a large bowl, whisk together eggs and egg yolks. Whisk in brown sugar. Add milk, vanilla and bourbon, if using, whisking well. Pour mixture over banana slices.

3. Bake in preheated oven for about 50 minutes or until pudding is puffed and center is firm to the touch. Let cool slightly before serving.

Chocolate Chip Raspberry Clafouti

Serves 8

Can you say clafouti without smiling? The Moosewood Restaurant Book of Desserts *inspired this recipe. It is a great dessert that makes me think of summertime.*

Preheat oven to 350°F (180°C)
10-inch (25 cm) deep-dish glass pie plate, greased

2 cups	fresh raspberries	500 mL
½ cup	semisweet chocolate chips	125 mL
4	eggs	4
¾ cup	all-purpose flour	175 mL
½ cup	granulated sugar	125 mL
½ cup	whipping (35%) cream	125 mL
½ cup	milk	125 mL
½ tsp	almond extract	2 mL

1. Scatter raspberries and chocolate chips in bottom of prepared pie plate.

2. In a blender or using an immersion/stick blender, combine eggs, flour, sugar, cream, milk and almond extract. Blend until smooth.

3. Pour batter over raspberries and chocolate chips. Bake in preheated oven for 55 to 60 minutes or until puffed, golden and a knife inserted into center comes out clean. Let cool for 15 minutes before serving.

Chocolate Chip Trifle

Serves about 20

This is a spectacular dessert that is really quite easy to assemble. Instant pudding tastes homemade with the addition of half-and-half cream and almond syrup. You can prepare this dessert a day ahead of time, which only improves the flavors and textures.

Tips

If unsweetened raspberries are unavailable, use frozen sweetened raspberries instead, but reduce the amount of sugar in the sauce to taste.

Almond syrup can be found in the coffee aisle of most large supermarkets.

Variation

Garnish the trifle with fresh raspberries.

Large glass bowl

12 oz	frozen unsweetened raspberries, thawed and including juice (about 3 cups/750 mL)	375 g
½ cup	superfine sugar	125 mL
⅔ cup	water	150 mL
2	boxes (each 3.4 oz/192 g) instant vanilla pudding mix	2
2 cups	milk	500 mL
1½ cups	half-and-half (10%) cream	375 mL
1 tsp	almond syrup (see Tips, left)	5 mL
8 cups	cake cubes (either pound or angel food cake)	2 L
¼ cup	sherry	50 mL
½ cup	semisweet chocolate chips	125 mL
1 cup	whipping (35%) cream	250 mL
1 tbsp	confectioner's (icing) sugar	15 mL
½ tsp	vanilla	2 mL

1. In a food processor fitted with a metal blade, pulse raspberries and sugar until berries are puréed. Strain mixture into a bowl, discarding solids. Whisk in water and set aside.

2. In a large bowl, whisk together instant pudding mixes, milk, half-and-half and almond syrup until smooth.

3. In bottom of a large glass bowl, arrange one-third of the cake cubes. Drizzle cake with one-third of the sherry, then one-third of the raspberry sauce. Sprinkle with one-third of the chocolate chips, then one-third of the custard. Repeat layers twice, ending with custard. Cover and refrigerate for several hours or overnight.

4. Before serving, in a large bowl with electric mixer or whisk, whip together cream, sugar and vanilla until soft peaks form. Spread on top of custard layer.

Old-Fashioned Dark Chocolate Pudding

You will love the old-fashioned chocolate hominess of this dessert. Just the name conjures images of comfort in Bubbie's kitchen.

Tip
You will find it easiest to cook this pudding in a heavy-bottomed nonstick saucepan.

½ cup	unsweetened Dutch-process cocoa powder, sifted	125 mL
⅓ cup	cornstarch	75 mL
¼ tsp	salt	1 mL
2 cups	milk	500 mL
2 cups	half-and-half (10%) cream	500 mL
¾ cup	granulated sugar	175 mL
1 cup	semisweet chocolate chips	250 mL
2 tsp	vanilla, divided	10 mL
1 cup	whipping (35%) cream	250 mL
2 tbsp	confectioner's (icing) sugar	25 mL

1. In a medium bowl, combine cocoa powder, cornstarch and salt.

2. In a large saucepan over medium-high heat, heat milk, half-and-half and sugar until sugar is dissolved. Quickly whisk in cocoa powder mixture until completely dissolved with no lumps. Reduce heat to medium and cook, stirring constantly, until thickened. Continue cooking and stirring for 2 minutes longer or until thickened. Remove from heat. Stir in chocolate chips and 1 tsp (5 mL) of the vanilla. Pour pudding into large bowl or six individual dishes.

3. Press a sheet of plastic wrap directly on surface of pudding to prevent a skin from forming. Let cool for 20 minutes. Refrigerate for several hours or until chilled, or overnight.

4. Meanwhile, in a medium bowl, using electric mixer, whip together cream, confectioner's sugar and remaining vanilla until soft peaks form.

5. Remove plastic wrap. Serve pudding with whipped cream.

Chocolate Caramel Sauce (*page 166*)

Chocolate Tapioca for Grown-Ups

I love comforting tapioca pudding. I call this recipe a grown-up version because it has a swift kick of Irish Cream — sure to help cure what ails ya!

Tips

You will find it easiest to cook this pudding in a heavy-bottomed nonstick saucepan. A great way to serve the pudding is in martini glasses garnished with a dollop of freshly whipped cream.

Small, airline-size bottles of liqueur are exactly ¼ cup (50 mL).

Variation

Substitute another sweet liqueur for the Irish Cream. Try Amaretto or Kahlúa for an equally pleasing flavor.

3 cups	milk	750 mL
½ cup	granulated sugar	125 mL
3 tbsp plus 1 tsp	quick-cooking tapioca	50 mL
2	egg yolks	2
1 cup	semisweet chocolate chips	250 mL
¼ cup	Irish Cream liqueur	50 mL
½ tsp	vanilla	2 mL

1. In a large saucepan, whisk together milk, sugar, tapioca and egg yolks. Let stand for 5 minutes.

2. Place saucepan over medium-high heat and cook, stirring constantly, until mixture is thickened and comes to a boil (it will look like bubbling lava). Cook for 2 minutes longer. Remove from heat and stir in chocolate chips, Irish Cream liqueur and vanilla. Scoop pudding into a large bowl or individual cups. Press a sheet of plastic wrap directly on surface to prevent a skin from forming. Let cool for 20 minutes. Refrigerate until chilled.

3. Remove plastic wrap. Serve pudding warm or chilled. The pudding will continue to thicken as it chills. It is best eaten the day it is made.

Chocolate Fondue *(page 171)*

Chocolate Cherry Terrine

Chocolate paradise would be a better name for this awesome dessert. The brandy-soaked cherries are draped with chocolate cream for a truly grand finale.

Tip

Garnish with a dollop of raspberry sorbet, if desired. For a decorative touch, lightly dust the serving plates with either unsweetened cocoa powder or confectioner's sugar.

9-by 5-inch (2 L) loaf pan, lined with plastic wrap

$3/4$ cup	dried sour cherries	175 mL
$1/4$ cup	cherry brandy	50 mL
4 cups	semisweet chocolate chips	1 L
2 oz	unsweetened chocolate, chopped	60 g
2 cups	whipping (35%) cream	500 mL

1. In a microwave-safe bowl, combine dried cherries and cherry brandy. Microwave on High for 40 seconds, just until heated. Set aside.

2. In a large microwave-safe bowl, combine chocolate chips, unsweetened chocolate and cream. Microwave on High for 3 to $3^1/_2$ minutes, stirring every 30 seconds, until chocolate is shiny and almost melted. Stir until smooth.

3. Whisk reserved cherry mixture into chocolate mixture. Spread in prepared pan. Cover and refrigerate overnight or until firm, or for up to 1 day.

4. Invert terrine onto a serving plate. Slice and serve.

Chocolate Tiramisu

The name of this fabulous Italian dessert means "pick-me-up." Be forewarned: once you make this dessert for guests, you will forever be known for it. My sister-in-law Meredith loves this dessert so much that she had me make giant ones for her wedding reception.

Tip

This dessert is best made 1 day before serving.

13-by 9-inch (3 L) glass baking dish or large bowl

2	packages (each 8 oz/250 g) cream cheese or mascarpone	2
2 cups	confectioner's (icing) sugar, sifted	500 mL
2⅓ cups	whipping (35%) cream	575 mL
1 cup	hot strong brewed coffee	250 mL
¾ cup	semisweet chocolate chips	175 mL
¼ cup	dark rum	50 mL
48	crisp ladyfingers, divided	48
	Unsweetened cocoa powder	

1. In a large bowl, using electric mixer, whip cream cheese until smooth. Add confectioner's sugar, whipping until creamy and smooth. With machine on low, gradually add cream in a steady stream. Whip mixture on high speed until it reaches soft peaks.

2. In a medium bowl, whisk together hot coffee, chocolate chips and rum until smooth. Dip half of the ladyfingers in coffee mixture and place in an even layer in bottom of baking dish. Spread half of the cream mixture over ladyfingers. Dip remaining ladyfingers in coffee mixture and place over cream mixture. Spread remaining cream mixture over ladyfingers, smoothing top.

3. Cover and refrigerate tiramisu overnight. Just before serving, lightly dust top with unsweetened cocoa powder.

Pumpkin Chip Bread Pudding

This dessert is a cross between pumpkin pie and bread pudding — delicious and comforting year-round. For an extra treat, drizzle caramel sauce across the top.

Preheat oven to 350°F (180°C)
13-by 9-inch (3 L) glass baking dish, greased

6 cups	lightly packed bread cubes (about 8 standard slices)	1.5 L
4	eggs	4
2½ cups	milk	625 mL
1¾ cups	pumpkin purée (not pie filling)	425 mL
¾ cup	granulated sugar	175 mL
¼ cup	packed dark brown sugar	50 mL
1 tsp	ground cinnamon	5 mL
½ tsp	ground allspice	2 mL
1 tsp	vanilla	5 mL
¾ cup	semisweet chocolate chips	175 mL

1. Place bread cubes in prepared dish and set aside.

2. In a large bowl, whisk together eggs, milk, pumpkin, granulated sugar, brown sugar, cinnamon, allspice and vanilla until combined. Pour mixture over bread cubes and sprinkle with chocolate chips. With a spatula, lightly press bread cubes and chocolate chips into custard mixture to coat.

3. Bake in preheated oven for 50 minutes or until top is puffed and center is firm to the touch. Let cool slightly before serving.

Sweet Endings

Chocolate Caramel Sauce

This decadent sauce goes together in a snap. From beginning to end, it takes only five minutes to prepare (quicker than running to the store). It's great served warm over ice cream.

Tips

For a fun fondue, serve this sauce warm with fruit, small cookies and cake cubes.

Store in a covered container in the refrigerator for up to 1 week.

Variation

You can omit the chocolate chips for an equally delicious caramel sauce. Use in recipes that call for caramel sauce.

¼ cup	unsalted butter	50 mL
¾ cup	packed light brown sugar	175 mL
⅓ cup	light corn syrup	75 mL
¼ tsp	salt	1 mL
⅓ cup	whipping (35%) cream	75 mL
⅓ cup	semisweet chocolate chips	75 mL

1. In a medium saucepan, melt butter over medium heat. Add brown sugar, corn syrup and salt. Increase heat to medium-high and bring mixture to a boil, stirring constantly. Once boiling, it will look like bubbling lava. Boil for 1 minute and remove from heat.

2. Whisk in cream. Add chocolate chips, whisking until smooth. The sauce will look as if it's separating but will smooth out after a minute or so of whisking. Sauce will thicken as it cools.

Chocolate Cherry Truffles

Makes about 36 truffles

You no longer have to go to fancy chocolate shops when you yearn for truffles. This very easy and decadent recipe will have you making truffles year-round. And, for an added bonus, they make a fabulous hostess gift.

Baking sheet, lined with waxed or parchment paper

2 cups	semisweet chocolate chips	500 mL
3/4 cup	whipping (35%) cream	175 mL
3/4 cup	dried sour cherries, finely chopped	175 mL
2 tbsp	Kirsch (cherry brandy)	25 mL
1/2 cup	unsweetened Dutch-process cocoa powder, sifted	125 mL

1. In a microwave-safe bowl, combine chocolate chips and cream. Microwave on High for 2 to $2\frac{1}{2}$ minutes, stirring every 30 seconds, until chocolate is shiny and almost melted. Stir until smooth.

2. Add dried cherries and Kirsch, stirring well. Refrigerate until firm. Scoop the chilled mixture by tablespoons (15 mL) and form into balls. Roll in unsweetened cocoa powder. Place on prepared baking sheet. Refrigerate truffles until ready to serve. Store in a covered container for up to 1 week.

Chocolate Toffee Crackers

Makes about 24 crackers

This recipe was given to me by my mother, who got it from her friend Mary Jo. This is my adaptation of the original. It has been given two very enthusiastic thumbs up from everyone who has tried it. A word of warning, though: this dessert is very habit forming!

Variation

Sprinkle chopped nuts over the chocolate.

Preheat oven to 350°F (180°C)
Rimmed baking sheet, lined with foil and greased

35 to 40	saltine soda crackers	35 to 40
1 cup	butter	250 mL
1 cup	packed light brown sugar	250 mL
2 cups	semisweet chocolate chips	500 mL
2 tbsp	shortening	25 mL

1. Arrange crackers in rows on prepared baking sheet right next to each other. The amount you use will depend upon dimensions of pan.

2. In a microwave-safe bowl, microwave butter on High until melted, about $1\frac{1}{2}$ minutes. Add brown sugar and stir. Microwave for 3 minutes longer, whisking every 30 seconds, until sugar is dissolved.

3. Whisk butter mixture until smooth and pour over crackers in pan. Bake in preheated oven until bubbling but not burning, about 14 to 17 minutes.

4. In a separate microwave-safe bowl, combine chocolate chips and shortening. Microwave on High for 2 to $2\frac{1}{2}$ minutes, stirring every 30 seconds, until chocolate is shiny and almost melted. Stir until smooth. Drizzle over cooled crackers. Refrigerate for 1 hour. Break into pieces. Store in an airtight container for up to 3 days.

Chocolate Crunchies

Makes about 30 crunchies

Ellen Bloom shared this recipe with my brother, Jon, who then passed it on to me. She says that these no-bake treats are her family's favorite. Taste them and you will see why.

Variation

Substitute 2 crushed peanut butter candy bars for the English toffee bits.

Baking sheet, lined with waxed or parchment paper

2 cups	semisweet chocolate chips	500 mL
2 tbsp	shortening	25 mL
8 oz	Chinese noodles	250 g
1 cup	English toffee candy bits	250 mL
$\frac{1}{2}$ cup	raisins (optional)	125 mL
	Confectioner's (icing) sugar	

1. In a large microwave-safe bowl, combine chocolate chips and shortening. Microwave on High for 2 to $2\frac{1}{2}$ minutes, stirring every 30 seconds, until chocolate is shiny and almost melted. Stir until smooth. Mix in Chinese noodles, toffee bits and raisins, if using. Mix well.

2. Using two spoons, drop mounds of chocolate mixture on prepared baking sheet, 1 to 2 inches (2.5 to 5 cm) apart. Sprinkle lightly with confectioner's sugar.

3. Refrigerate chocolate mounds until firm. When hardened, carefully peel off waxed paper. Store in an airtight container in the refrigerator if the weather is warm so the chocolate doesn't melt.

Chocolate-Dipped Pretzels

Makes 12 pretzels

I love to get children involved in the kitchen. This is a perfect cooking project because it's easy to do, gives quick results and tastes great. My children use these as bartering chips at school.

Variation

Substitute dried fruit or unseasoned potato chips for the pretzels.

Baking sheet, lined with waxed or parchment paper

1 cup	semisweet chocolate chips	250 mL
1 tbsp	shortening	15 mL
12	pretzel rods	12
	Assorted sprinkles, candies or chopped nuts for sprinkling	

1. In a microwave-safe bowl, combine chocolate chips and shortening. Microwave on High for 1 to 2 minutes, stirring every 30 seconds, until chocolate is shiny and almost melted. Stir until smooth.

2. Dip top halves of pretzel rods in melted chocolate. Place on prepared baking sheet. Sprinkle chocolate-covered halves with sprinkles, candies or nuts.

3. Refrigerate until chocolate is hardened. Remove from refrigerator and transfer to an airtight container. Store at room temperature for up to 2 days.

Chocolate Fondue

*Chocolate fondue is a very
elegant dessert. It is so easy
to make that you shouldn't
let others know exactly how
easy. It is a very special
dessert for a child's birthday
when made without the
liqueur; you can substitute
decaf coffee instead.*

Tips

Leftover fondue can be
refrigerated overnight. Warm
in microwave before serving.

Try to use a fondue pot with
a tea light that is made for
chocolate fondue so that
the chocolate won't burn.

Ceramic fondue pot or medium ceramic dish

¾ cup	whipping (35%) cream	175 mL
1 cup	semisweet chocolate chips	250 mL
2 tbsp	liqueur such as hazelnut or Galliano	25 mL

Suggested Dipping Items

Cubes of loaf or pound cake

Strawberries

Banana chunks

Orange segments

Pretzels

Large marshmallows

Small cookies

Dried fruit

1. In a microwave-safe bowl, combine cream and chocolate chips. Microwave on High for 1 to 2 minutes, stirring every 30 seconds, until chocolate is shiny and almost melted. Stir until smooth.

2. Whisk liqueur into chocolate mixture. Transfer to fondue pot.

3. Arrange dipping items on a platter and serve.

Chocolate Merlot Sauce

**Makes 1⅓ cups
(325 mL)**

*This is an outrageous sauce.
Complex and simple at the
same time, it takes only a
couple of minutes to prepare.
You will want to use this on
everything you eat — although
I wouldn't necessarily
recommend it!*

Tip

Serve drizzled over ice cream,
sorbet or chocolate cake.

Variation

Substitute Cabernet
Sauvignon for the Merlot.

1 cup	semisweet chocolate chips	250 mL
½ cup	Merlot wine	125 mL
⅓ cup	light corn syrup	75 mL

1. In a medium saucepan, combine chocolate chips,
wine and corn syrup. Warm over medium heat,
whisking constantly, just until chocolate is melted.
Remove from heat and whisk until smooth.

Chocolate Rum Balls

These rum balls were a huge hit last holiday season. After I served them to friends, my phone began to ring off the hook with demands for the recipe. We like to eat them year-round.

Variation

Substitute pecans for the walnuts and dried cranberries for the apricots.

12 oz	vanilla wafer cookies (about 86 cookies)	375 g
1 cup	walnuts	250 mL
1 cup	semisweet chocolate chips	250 mL
3/4 cup	dried apricots	175 mL
1/2 cup	confectioner's (icing) sugar, sifted	125 mL
1/2 cup	dark rum	125 mL
3 tbsp	light corn syrup	45 mL
2 tbsp	unsweetened Dutch-process cocoa powder	25 mL
	Unsweetened Dutch-process cocoa powder, sifted	
	Confectioner's (icing) sugar, sifted	

1. In a food processor fitted with a metal blade, process cookies until finely ground. Transfer to a large bowl. Add walnuts and chocolate chips to processor, pulsing until finely chopped. Add to cookie crumbs. Process dried apricots in processor until finely chopped. Add to cookie mixture.

2. Add confectioner's sugar, rum, corn syrup and cocoa powder to cookie mixture, stirring well. Scoop dough with a spoon and form into 1-inch (2.5 cm) balls. Roll in unsweetened cocoa powder. Store rum balls in an airtight container at room temperature for up to 1 week. Before serving, roll in confectioner's sugar.

Chocolate Strawberry Syrup

*This quick sauce is great
drizzled on pancakes or
French toast or spooned over
vanilla ice cream. Served
warm or cold, this is a winner.*

Tip
This syrup is best served
the day it is made.

10 oz	frozen unsweetened strawberries, thawed and including juice (about 2½ cups/625 mL)	300 g
⅓ cup	superfine sugar	75 mL
1 cup	semisweet chocolate chips	250 mL
⅓ cup	water	75 mL
2 tsp	Triple Sec or other orange-flavored liqueur	10 mL

1. In a processor fitted with a metal blade, pulse strawberries and sugar until smooth. Pour blended strawberries into a microwave-safe bowl. Add chocolate chips and microwave on High for 1 to 2 minutes, stirring every 30 seconds, until chocolate is shiny and almost melted. Stir until smooth.

2. Whisk sauce until smooth. If chocolate isn't completely melted, microwave for 20 seconds longer. Whisk in water and liqueur.

Quick Cinnamon Chocolate Pastries

Makes about 36 pastries

I have always loved the chocolate chip pastries that you find in delicatessens, but unfortunately they are very time-consuming to make. I wanted to develop a recipe that packs the similar chocolate chip cinnamon goodness of those deli treats without the labor. I came up with this dessert, which is quick, easy and delicious.

Tip

These pastries look great sprinkled with confectioner's (icing) sugar. They are wonderful served with coffee or as an accompaniment to homemade ice cream.

Preheat oven to 425°F (220°C)
Baking sheets, lined with parchment paper

1	package (17.3 oz/490 g) frozen puff pastry sheets (about 9½ inches/24 cm square) or 1 package (13 oz/397 g) block puff pastry	1
½ cup	granulated sugar	125 mL
½ tsp	ground cinnamon	2 mL
⅔ cup	miniature semisweet chocolate chips	150 mL

1. Thaw puff pastry at room temperature for 30 minutes or according to package directions.

2. In a small bowl, combine sugar and cinnamon.

3. If pastry is a block, cut in half. On a floured surface, roll out each half to 9½-inch (24 cm) square sheets. Working with one sheet at a time, sprinkle half of the cinnamon sugar over top, then half of the miniature chocolate chips, leaving ½-inch (1 cm) bare at one edge. Brush bare edge with water. Starting at edge opposite, tightly roll up pastry jelly roll style, gently pressing to help chocolate chips adhere and pinching edge to seal. Repeat with remaining sheet of pastry. Slice into ½-inch (1 cm) thick slices, carefully placing rounds cut side up on prepared baking sheets, about 1 inch (2.5 cm) apart. (Don't worry if some sugar or chocolate chips fall out. Just sprinkle them on top or tuck them back into pastry slice.)

4. Bake in preheated oven for 19 to 22 minutes or until medium brown and crisp. The pastries will look somewhat caramelized on top. Let cool completely on pan on rack. Store in an airtight container for up to 2 days.

Hip Chip Trail Mix

**Makes about
3½ cups (875 mL)**

*Whip up this delicious
combination of caramelized
pecans, salted almonds,
chocolate chips and tangy
dried apricots in a jiffy. Try
not to make it too far in
advance of serving as the
caramelized nuts can get
sticky. Serve with mint tea
or strong coffee.*

Tip

Trail mix is best served the
day it is made (it tends to
get too sticky).

Baking sheet, lined with parchment paper or foil

1 cup	whole pecans	250 mL
⅓ cup	granulated sugar	75 mL
1 cup	dry roasted salted almonds	250 mL
1 cup	dried apricots, snipped into slivers (see Tip, page 36)	250 mL
½ cup	semisweet chocolate chips	125 mL
Pinch	salt	Pinch

1. In a large nonstick skillet over medium-high heat, toast pecans, stirring often, until they just start to turn golden, about 5 minutes.

2. Reduce heat to medium-high. Add sugar, stirring or shaking the pan as necessary, until sugar is melted, about 5 minutes. If sugar or nuts start to burn, reduce heat to low.

3. Spread caramelized nuts on prepared baking sheet, separating pecans with a fork as necessary. Be careful not to burn your fingers as caramel is very hot. Let pecans cool completely on pan on rack.

4. In a medium bowl, combine cooled pecans, almonds, dried apricots and chocolate chips. Sprinkle with salt and serve.

Mocha Fudge Sauce

Makes 3½ cups (875 mL)

This beats store-bought fudge sauce any day! I thought that a coffee-based sauce with a chewy fudge flavor would be dynamite over ice cream. I realized that I was on to something when my husband started eating the sauce with a spoon.

Tip
This sauce can be made ahead. Simply cover and refrigerate cooled sauce. Reheat in the microwave until warm and melted.

Variation
Use a flavored liqueur in place of the rum. Kirsch and crème de menthe work well.

1 cup	unsweetened Dutch-process cocoa powder, sifted	250 mL
½ cup	packed light brown sugar	125 mL
1 cup	hot freshly brewed coffee	250 mL
½ cup	whipping (35%) cream	125 mL
½ cup	light corn syrup	125 mL
2 cups	semisweet chocolate chips	500 mL
2 tbsp	dark rum	25 mL

1. In a large saucepan, whisk together cocoa powder and brown sugar. Add coffee, cream and corn syrup, whisking until smooth.

2. Bring to a boil over medium-high heat, whisking continuously. Remove from heat and whisk in chocolate chips and rum.

3. Let cool and thicken slightly before serving over ice cream. Cover and refrigerate any leftover sauce for up to 2 days.

Quick-Mix Chocolate Fudge

This fudge is delectable, known to make even the most jaded fudge lovers swoon. Until this recipe, I was never a huge fudge lover. Now I am president of the fudge fan club.

Variation

Substitute your favorite liqueur for the Galliano.

8-inch (2 L) square baking pan, greased

2½ cups	semisweet chocolate chips	625 mL
3 oz	unsweetened chocolate, chopped	90 g
1⅓ cups	sweetened condensed milk	325 mL
¼ tsp	salt	1 mL
¼ cup	Galliano liqueur	50 mL

1. In a medium saucepan, combine chocolate chips, unsweetened chocolate, sweetened condensed milk and salt. Cook over medium-low heat, stirring constantly. Chocolate mixture will be very thick and hard to stir, but keep stirring so that chocolate doesn't burn.

2. When chocolate is almost melted, turn off burner. Continue stirring over warm burner until chocolate is completely melted. Stir in liqueur, mixing until smooth.

3. Spread chocolate mixture in prepared pan, smoothing top with a spatula. Cover and refrigerate for about 2 hours or until firm. Cut into 16 squares.

Rocky Roads

I love the fact that you can make these gems in five minutes flat. If you are in a really big hurry (with only a few minutes before your guests arrive), place Rocky Roads in the freezer instead of the refrigerator. Freeze for about 15 minutes or until firm.

Variations

Substitute toasted hazelnuts for almonds.

You can also add $\frac{1}{2}$ cup (125 mL) dried sour cherries to the Rocky Roads.

Baking sheet, lined with waxed or parchment paper

$2\frac{3}{4}$ cups	semisweet chocolate chips	675 mL
2 tbsp	shortening	25 mL
1 cup	almonds, toasted (see Tips, page 33)	250 mL
6 oz	miniature marshmallows (about 5 cups/1.25 L)	175 g

1. In a large microwave-safe bowl, combine chocolate chips and shortening. Microwave on High for 2 to $2\frac{1}{2}$ minutes, stirring every 30 seconds, until chocolate is shiny and almost melted. Stir until smooth. If chocolate mixture is hot, let cool until slightly warm.

2. Stir almonds and marshmallows into chocolate mixture. Using two spoons, scoop mounds of mixture onto prepared baking sheet. Refrigerate until chocolate is firm. Store in an airtight container for up to 2 days.

Strawberry Cheesecake Mousse Parfaits

A version of this dessert won our bakery the coveted Best Dessert Chef's Affair 2000 award. We serve it in martini glasses with graham cracker crumbs and raspberry sauce.

Variation

Top the parfaits with chocolate sandwich crumbs instead of graham cracker crumbs, if desired.

4	whole graham crackers	4
10 oz	frozen unsweetened strawberries, thawed and including liquid (about 2½ cups/625 mL)	300 g
⅓ cup	superfine sugar	75 mL
⅓ cup	water	75 mL
1	package (8 oz/250 g) cream cheese, softened	1
1 cup	confectioner's (icing) sugar	250 mL
1¼ cups	whipping (35%) cream	300 mL
1 tbsp	gold rum (optional)	15 mL
¾ cup	semisweet chocolate chips	175 mL

1. In a food processor fitted with a metal blade, pulse graham crackers until finely ground. Transfer to a bowl and set aside. Wipe out processor bowl.

2. Place strawberries in clean processor. Pulse just until chunky. Transfer strawberries to a separate bowl. Whisk in sugar and water. Set aside.

3. In a separate bowl, using electric mixer, whip cream cheese until smooth. Add confectioner's sugar, whipping until creamy and smooth. Gradually add cream and rum in a steady stream, beating on low speed. Whisk mixture on high speed until it reaches soft peaks.

4. Place a scoop of the cream cheese mixture in each of six wine glasses. Drizzle with some of the strawberry sauce and sprinkle with chocolate chips. Continue layering cream cheese mixture, strawberry sauce and chocolate chips until glasses are three-quarters full. Top each parfait with about 1 tbsp (15 mL) of the graham cracker crumbs.

Dark Chocolate Syrup

Since most of us probably have a can or two of chocolate syrup in our fridge, you might think it crazy to make it from scratch. But after just one taste, you will be convinced. This delectably delicious syrupy sauce goes together in minutes and will bring out your deepest chocoholic tendencies.

Tip

The syrup is fabulous stirred into milk, soy milk or hot coffee. It also tastes great drizzled over ice cream. It will keep, refrigerated, for at least 1 week. If refrigerated chocolate syrup becomes slightly grainy, warm briefly in microwave before using.

Variation

Stir 1 tsp (5 mL) orange zest into the hot syrup for an out-of-this-world taste.

2 cups	water	500 mL
1½ cups	granulated sugar	375 mL
1 cup	unsweetened Dutch-process cocoa powder, sifted	250 mL
2 tsp	instant coffee granules	10 mL
½ cup	semisweet chocolate chips	125 mL
2 tsp	vanilla	10 mL

1. In a large saucepan over medium-high heat, whisk together water and sugar. Heat mixture for about 5 minutes, whisking occasionally, until hot and sugar is dissolved. Whisk in cocoa powder and instant coffee. Simmer for 2 minutes. Remove from heat.

2. Add chocolate chips to saucepan, whisking until smooth. Whisk in vanilla.

3. Let syrup cool to room temperature. Use immediately or store in refrigerator until ready to use.

National Library of Canada Cataloguing in Publication

Hasson, Julie
    125 best chocolate chip recipes / Julie Hasson.

Includes index.
ISBN 0-7788-0072-5

1. Cookery (Chocolate). I. Title. II. Title: One hundred
twenty-five best chocolate chip recipes.

TX767.C5H38 2003   641.6'374   C2003-901330-8

Index